ENCYCLOPAEDIA OF INDIAN GOVERNMENT: PROGRAMMES AND POLICIES

ENCYCLOPAEDIA OF INDIAN GOVERNMENT: PROGRAMMES AND POLICIES

Vol. 30

Social Justice and Empowerment

Edited by

Satish Tiwari

ANMOL PUBLICATIONS PVT. LTD.

NEW DELHI - 110 002 (INDIA)

ANMOL PUBLICATIONS PVT. LTD.
4374/4B, Ansari Road, Daryaganj
New Delhi - 110 002

Encyclopaedia of Indian Government: Programmes and Policies

First Edition, 2000
ISBN 81-261-0515-1 (Set)

PRINTED IN INDIA

Published by J.L. Kumar for Anmol Publications Pvt. Ltd., New Delhi - 110 002 and Printed at Mehra Offset Press, Delhi.

Contents

Preface

Encyclopaedia of Indian Government: Programmes and Policies contains authoritative information on about fifty departmental policies and their future developmental programmes.

Organised to be completed in 40 volumes, this gigantic work covers Agriculture; Atomic Energy; Chemicals and Fertilizers; Coal; Commerce; Communication; Culture; Defence; Education; Environment and Forests; External Affairs; Finance; Food & Consumer Affairs; Food Processing Industries; Health and Family Welfare; Home Affairs and Internal Security; Human Resources; Industry; Information and Broadcasting; Labour; Law, Justice and Company Affairs; Non-conventional Energy Sources; Ocean Development; Parliamentary Affairs; Personnel, Public Grievances and Pensions; Petroleum and Natural Gas; Planning and Programme Implementation; Planning and Statistics; Posts and Telegraphs; Power; Rural Development; Science and Technology; Social Justice and Empowerment; Space; States Affairs; Steel; Steel and Mines; Sugar and Edible Oils; Surface Transport; Textiles; Tourism; Urban Development; Water Resources; Women and Child development etc.

Based on the information derived from authoritative sources, this work contains authentic facts and figures. I am deeply beholden to all the scholars whose writings are cited or substantially made use of in the present work. I am also thankful to Anmol Publications Pvt. Ltd for undertaking publication of this encyclopaedia. I am solely responsible for shortcomings in presentation of matter.

Encyclopaedic in nature, this will prove a dependable reference work for scholars and academics besides those appearing for different competitive examinations.

—**Satish Tiwari**

1

Introduction

The following subjects which fall within list one of the Seventh Schedule to the Constitution of India:

1. Operation of Indo-US, Indo-UK, Indo-German, Indo-Swiss and Indo-Swedish Agreements for duty-free receipt of donated relief supplies, goods and matters connected with the distribution of supplies and coming thereunder.

The following subjects which fall within List III of the Seventh Schedule to the Constitution of India (as regards legislation) only.

2. Social Security and Social Insurance save to the extent allotted to any other Department.

For the Union Territories, the following subjects which fall within List 11 or List I of the Seventh Schedule to the Constitution of India in so far as they exist in regard to such Territories.

3. Relief to the disable and unemployable and measures relating to social security and social insurance, save to the extent allotted to any other Department.

General and consequentials

4. Social Welfare, Social Welfare Planning, Project

formulation, Research, Evaluation, Statistics and Training.

5. Conventions with other countries in matters relating to Social Defence and references from United Nations Organisation relating to prevention of crime and treatment of offenders.
6. Institutional and non-institutional services in the care and development of children and aged.
7. Education, Training, Rehabilitation and Welfare of physically and mentally handicapped.
8. National Institute for the Physically Handicapped and Mentally Retarded.
9. National Centre for the Blind including Central Braille Press, Dehradun, Training Centre for the Adult Deaf and School for the partially deaf children, Hyderabad, Model School for Mentally Retarded Children, New Delhi, and other National Institutes.
10. Social and Moral Hygienic Programme.
11. Beggary, Juvenile Vagrancy, Delinquency and other CARE Programme.
12. Probation of Juvenile offenders.
13. Research, Evaluation, Training, exchange of information and technical guidance on all Social Defence matters including correctional services.
14. All matters relating to prohibition.
15. Educational and Social Welfare aspects of drug addiction.
16. Charitable and religious endowments pertaining to subjects allocated to this Ministry.
17. Promotion and development of voluntary effort on subject allocated to this Ministry.
18. National Institute of Social Defence.

19. Artificial Limbs Manufacturing Corporation of India, Kanpur (ALIMCO)
20. All other attached or subordinate offices and other organisations concerned with any of the subjects specified in this list.
21. Administration of following Acts:
    (a) Prohibition of Offenders Act, 1958
    (b) Children Act, 1960
22. Scheduled Castes, Scheduled Tribes Denotified/ Nomadic and Semi-Nomadic tribes and Other Backward Classes including scholarships to students belonging to such Castes, Tribes and Classes.
23. (a) Appointment, resignation of Chairperson, Vice-Chairperson and Members of National Commission for asstes and Scheduled Tribes.
    (c) Appointment of Chairperson, Vice-Chairperson and Members of the National Commission for Safai Karamcharis; and
    (d) Reports of the National Commission for Safai Karamcharis
24. Development of Scheduled Castes and Scheduled Tribes.
25. (a) Implementation of the Supreme Court Judgement in the Indira Sawhney & Other Vs. Union of India (Mandal case) providing reservation to other Backward Classes (OBCs) in Central Govt., jobs.
    (b) Administration of the National Commission of Backward Classes, Act, 1993.
    (c) Matters relating to the National Backward Classes Finance and Development Corporation (NBCFDC)

26. (a) Scheduled Areas
    (b) Matters relating to autonomous districts of Assam excluding roads and bridge works and ferries thereon; and
    (c) Regulation framed by the Governors of States for the Scheduled Areas and for tribal areas specified in Part-A of the Table appended to paragraph 20 of the Sixth Schedule to the Constitution.

27. (a) Commission to report on the administration of Scheduled Areas and Welfare of Scheduled Tribes; and
    (b) Issue of directions regarding drawing up and execution of Schemes essential for the welfare of Scheduled Tribes in any State.
    (c) Tribal Cooperative Marketing Development Federation of India Ltd, (TRIFIED)

28. (a) Appointment, resignation etc. of Special Officer for Linguistic Minorities.
    (b) Report of the Special Officer; and
    (c) All matters relating to Linguistic Minorities.

29. (a) National Commission for Minorities Act, 1992 and matters relating to National Commission for Minorities and Reports of the Commission;
    (b) 15-Point Programme for the Welfare Minorities and Other matters relating religious minorities.
    (c) National Minorities Development Finance Corporation and other welfare schemes for Minorities.

30. The WAKF Act, 1995 (43 of 1995)

31. Administration of WAKF properties under I Administration of Evacuee Property Act, 19 (31 of 1950).

32. Administration of Durgah Khawaja Saheb A 1955 (36 of 1955).
33. Representation of Anglo-Indian Community.
34. All matters relating to minority community accept matters relating to Law & Order.
35. (a) The Prevention of Cruelty to Animals Ai 1960 (59 of 1960).
    (b) The Prevention of Cruelty to Animals.

2

Policy and Approach

The Ministry of Social Justice and Empowerment is entrusted with the welfare, social justice and empowerment of disadvantaged and marginalised sections of the society viz., Scheduled Castes, Scheduled Tribes, Minorities, Backward Classes, Disabled, Aged persons, Street Children and victims Act, of Drug Abuse etc. During the Vth Plan period, a beginning was made to extend economic development parallel to social empowerment. This was resolved through viable institutions for extending credit at low interest to the families under double the Poverty Line.

The basic objectives of the policies, programmes, law and institutions of the Indian Welfare System is to bring the target groups into the mainstream of development by making them self reliant.

The Ninth Plan commits itself towards empowering SCs, STs, OBCs and Minorities as one of its nine primary objectives. While the ongoing programmes or these groups will be streamlined and strengthened, new measures will be taken, wherever necessary to accelerate the process of empowering these weaker sections. Empowerment will be attempted in an integrated manner, essentially, covering three vital components viz. (i) Social Empowerment (ii) Economic Empowerment and

(ii) Social justice Thus the approach will be holistic in nature to accomplish all round development with inter-sectorial approach and inputs from both Governmental and Non-Governmental agencies.

Keeping in view the approach & objective envisaged for the ninth five year plan, the, Ministry of Social Justice and Empowerment reviewed all the on going programmes and restructured most of them wherever necessary. In addition, many new measures were taken to strengthen participation by both Governmental & Non Governmental Agencies in extending benefits to the target groups.

Despite resource constraints, the commitment and constant endeavour of the Government has resulted in improvement of the educational status and representation in services both of SCs and STs to an appreciable level since independence. The Tribal Sub plan strategy and Special Central Assistance have yielded considerable improvement in the conditions of Scheduled Tribe population. Special efforts are being made to review the approach, methodology and coverage of ongoing programmes and take remedial measures for their effective implementation to improve the socioeconomic conditions of Scheduled Castes and Scheduled Tribes and Safai Karamcharis.

The State Governments look after the welfare and development of Scheduled Castes and Scheduled Tribes through their respective Special Component Plan with the support of Special Central Assistance provided by Central Government. The Central Government also participate in the share capital investment of the States Scheduled Castes/ Scheduled Tribes Finance and Development Corporations (SCDCs) who act as guarantors, promoters and catalysts for generating credit from financial institutions providing missing inputs by way of margin money loans and subsidy to the target groups. Besides, the National Scheduled Castes and Scheduled Tribes Finance and Development Corporation is assisting target-group by providing necessary funds at concessional rates to State level SCDCs and other channelising agencies for implementing various viable and feasible schemes/ projects.

A National Safai Karamcharis Finance and Development Corporation (NSKFDC) is functioning to promote economic development/self-employment for the economic rehabilitation of Safai Karamcharis besides providing training in technical and entrepreneural skills and extending loans to students from Safai Karamchari community for persuing higher education.

The Scheduled Castes and Scheduled Tribes (Prevention of Atrocities) Act, 1989 aims at preventing atrocities against the members of Scheduled Castes and Scheduled Tribes and to provide Special courts for trial of such offences and for the relief and rehabilitation of the victims of such offences and for matters connected therewith or incidental thereto.

As a follow up measure to Supreme Court's direction, 27% reservation in Government employment and relaxation for entrance in Competitive Examinations under the provisions of Article 16(4) of the constitution for the Backward Classes have been made since 1993. National Backward Classes Finance Development Corporation has established itself for providing necessary funds for Backward Classes for feasible self employment schemes.

Special attention is also focussed on effective implementation of the 15-point programme for the Welfare of Minorities. With the establishment of Maulana Azad Foundation and National Minorities Finance and Development Corporation, and the pre-examination coaching facilities, the minorities have got a new deal in self-employment oriented programme with concessional credit.

The Ministry have been providing rehabilitation services to the disabled persons in increasing measure through a number of schemes. These services include early detection, fitment of aids and appliances, educational, vocational and employment for the disabled population of the country.

A separate National Handicapped Finance and Development corporation has been incorporated on 24 January, 1997 to provide concessional finance for a wide range of activities including self-employment ventures, upgrading skill, assistance for infrastructural activities which support economic pursuits, loans for education etc. through State channelising agencies.

The greatest achievements is enactment of the comprehensive legislation called "Persons with Disabilities, Equal Opportunities, Protection of Rights and Full Participation Act 1995", to ensure prevention, care and rehabilitation of the disabled so that they get equal opportunities with full participation in nation building activities. The emphasis of the Ministry is to facilitate convergence approach reach out services to rural areas also through I community based programmes. NGOs play significant role as an integral parts of our resolve welfare services to the disabled.

Problems and issues of street children, drugs addicts, aged, juvenile delinquents and beggars a being addressed by way of providing specific grants to NGOs and encouraging State Governments and local bodies to come forward to take up their law with the financial assistance and other incentives made available. Demand reduction strategies at work places are also introduced through nod collaborative projects which have proved to successful in practical sense and ready for expansion through adoption/guardianship.

The work relating to the Animal Welfare he been transferred to this Ministry w.e.f. 3.9.98. Since then, the Ministry has launched two central sector schemes under which grants are being given to NGOs for providing medical assistance and shelter houses for animals. In addition three more scheme are awaiting approval of Planning Commission.

The Ministry continues to interact with the State Governments and other Ministries/Department of the Government of India, voluntary agencies and concerned International bodies in an increasing measure and will continue to struggle hard to achieve the goals set for the social justice and empowerment of the disadvantaged and marginalised sections of the society. The policy of the Ministry is to encourage participation of the community and maximum utilisation of existing infrastructure and voluntary action in its programme interventions.

3

Highlights of Achievements

Scheduled castes development

Ministry of Social Justice and Empowerment has taken a new initiative by removing the restriction of only two male children of a family being eligible under the Post Matric Scholarship Scheme for Scheduled Castes and Scheduled Tribes students. The committed liability contribution in this scheme has been waived off for North Eastern States. During 1998-99, an expenditure of Rs. 99.96 crore has been incurred under this Scheme benefitting 22 lakh student.

The Scheme of National Overseas Scholarships for Scheduled Castes and Sheduled Tribes, etc. has been improved upon and is being made functional from September, 1999 Session onwards. The maintenance allowance for researches has been increased from $6600 to $7700 per annum. The annual income ceiling for eligibility under the Scheme has been increased to Rs. 1,44,000/-.

A new thrust has been given to the Centrally Sponsored Scheme of hostels for Scheduled Castes girls and boys. Under the scheme, the non-Governmental Organisations, also get assistance through their State Government/UT Administrations for extension of their existing hostels. The Central universities being provided with financial assistance up to 90 per cent under the scheme whereas they are expected to contribute 10 per cent of the expenditure. Other universities are also eligible to receive central assistance up to 45 per cent of the total expenditure.

Under the scheme of aid to voluntary organisations, the procedures for sanctioning the grants have been simplified and the scope of the scheme has been expanded to include the programme of creating awareness regarding Government programmes like Human Rights, Consumer Protection and Environment as well as the facilities provided by Government. Special attention is being focussed to Scheduled Castes beneficiaries living in North Eastern Region and priority coverage is being provided for Scheduled Castes women.

The authorized share capital of National Scheduled Castes and Scheduled Tribes Finance and Development Corporation has been enhanced form Rs. 300 crores to Rs. 1000 crores during this year. The National Commission for Scheduled Castes and Scheduled Tribes has been reconstituted on 16.12.1998.

Tribal development

A new Central Sector Scheme for the development of Primitive Tribal Groups has been introduced during current financial year. Under this scheme cent percent assistance would be available to Integrated Tribal Development Projects (ITDPs), Tribal Research Institute (TRI) and Non-Governmental Organisations (NGOs) for undertaking activities such as awareness generation and confidence building, training for skill development of tribal youth organisations of self help groups and provision of services/Inputs; not covered by any existing scheme.

Scheduled areas and scheduled tribes commission: It has been decided to set up 11 member Scheduled Areas and

Scheduled Tribe Commission under Article 339(1) of the Constitution. The main objective of the Commission is to examine the existing Tribal Sub-Plan strategy and to suggest alternative arrangements if necessary.

National institute for training and research In tribal affairs: It has been decided to set up a National Institute for Training and Research in Tribal Affairs at Delhi. This Institute will serve as an apex body of the State level Tribal Research Institutes.

Revision of schemes have been initiated after consultation with the Planning Commission and the Ministry of Finance. Revision of norms of the Scheme of Grant-in-Aid to Voluntary Organisation working for the Welfare of the Scheduled Tribes have been made raising the cost heads to a realistic and workable level.

Grants under article 275(1) of the constitution (Setting up of residential schools): During the year 1997-98, it was decided to utilise a part of fund under the scheme for setting up 100 residential schools from Class 6 to 12 for tribal students. The objective of setting up of residential schools is to provide quality education to tribal students.

Welfare of other backward classes (OBCs)

The Following schemes have been launched for the welfare of OBCs during the Ninth Plan:-

- Scheme of Pre Examination Coaching for OBCs (Central Scheme);
- Hostels for OBCs Boys and Girls (Centrally Sponsored Scheme);
- Scheme of Pre-Matric Scholarships for OBCs (Centrally Sponsored Scheme);
- Scheme of Post-Matric Scholarships for OBCs for studies in India (100% Centrally Sponsored Scheme)
- Assistance to Voluntary Organisations for Welfare of OBCs (Central Scheme).

A Conference of State Secretaries Incharge of Backward Classes under the Chairmanship of Secretary, Social Justice and Empowerment was held on 4.12.98 to discuss specific issues and give thrust to the recently launched schemes for welfare of backward Classes. In order to provide higher degree of flexibility so that states can avail the benefits of the schemes in an effective manner, an Expert Group under Chairmanship of Joint Secretary (Minorities and Backward Classes) and the Secretaries-in-charge of Backward Classes Welfare of States of Bihar, Uttar Pradesh, Madhya Pradesh, Tamil Nadu, Andhra Pradesh, and Delhi was formed as decided in the meeting. This group held its first meeting on 22nd January, 1999 with the objective to have a re-look at the approved schemes of Backward Classes Division of this Ministry so that steps are taken for effective and quick implementation of the new schemes formulated by this Ministry for welfare of OBCs, the Group suggested some modification in the schemes.

Welfare of the minorities

Ministry of Social Justice & Empowerment has been implementing the scheme of Pre-examination coaching for weaker sections based on economic criteria since 1992-93 for the target group consisting of minorities whose income does not exceed Rs. 44,500/- P.A. with the objective to train the candidates belonging to the target groups, through the reputed coaching institutions to enable them to compete on equal terms with other candidates in the examinations leading to recruitment in government jobs and admission in professional courses. The scheme is being implemented through reputed coaching institutions. The scheme has been revised and DITs (Designated Inspection Teams) have been formed in the States. A sum of Rs. 1.09 crores has been sanctioned to 50 institutions upto the first week of February, 1999.

In pursuance of the strategy of area based approach for tackling the problems of Minorities, the scheme of multi-sectoral development plans has been launched during 1995-96 in 41 minorities, concentration districts. Under this scheme, the concerned States are required to undertake surveys and prepare project reports through an expert agency in respect of activities conspicuously pursued by the minorities in these districts with a view to identify the requirements of credit, marketing, training, technological support, etc. for carrying out such activities in a viable way. The Multi Sectoral Plans in respect 29 districts in 7 States have been prepared.

The Government of India has contributed to the equity share capital of the National Minorities Development & Finance Corporation (NMDFC) to the tune of As. 125 crores (i.e. 25% of the share capital of As. 500 crores of the Corporation). As on 31.1.99 NMDFC has disbursed As. 177.10 crores to 36914 beneficiaries.

The 15-Point Programme for welfare of minorities, drawn in 1983 is proposed to be recast so as to make it an effective instrument for ensuring non-discrimination against the minorities and to focus on the positive steps required to be taken to create a feeling of confidence among them.

Welfare of the disabled

1998 has been a year of new initiatives and all-round growth of the Disability Division. Grants-in-aid Schemes have been revised. Their scope enlarged and procedures simplified to make them more user friendly.

A Bilateral Agreement with NIDRR, Washington USA, was signed for transfer of technology. For the first time mentally challenged children participated in the Republic Day Parade at par with others and won the second prize.

Scope of the RCI was extended to include several other categories of professionals such as Physiotherapists, Occupational Therapists and Opthalmic Technicians. Bridge courses to train rehabilitiation workers were organised. Expenditure under Plan funds of the Division increased from Rs. 25.06 crores in 1992-93 (as on 31.33.1993) to Rs. 75.23 crores (as on 31.1.1999).

A National Pilot Programme for the integration of the mentally challenged persons in the society was launched. 10,3319 persons have been identified and integrated in six States. Ability India Exhibition was held exhibiting the entire reange of aids and appliance available in the country. The National handicapped Finance & Development Corporation sanctioned loans to 822 persons amounting to Rs. 3.41 crores.

Social defence

During the year an effort was made to streamline and update the policies and programmes of the Social Defence Division, particularly those relating to older persons and children. The National Institute of Social Defence (NISD) was also strengthened by improving the physical infrastructure of the Institute and by introducing new training programmes. The establishment of a Centre for Drug Abuse Prevention (C-DAP) within the institute has also been planned. Some of the major initiatives taken by the Division during the year include:

Preparation of a Plan of Action to observe 1999 as the International Year of Older Persons.

Announcement of a national policy for older persons

Revision of the Schemes of Assistance to Panchayati Raj Institutions/Voluntary Organisations/ Self Help Groups of construction of old age homes/multi service centres for older persons.

An Integrated Programme for Older Persons was launched by revising the existing scheme for older persons. Launch of an Old Age Social and Income Security (OASIS) Project to comprehensively examine policy issues relating to old age income security. The first part of the Expert Committee Report was presented to the Finance Minister by the Minister for Social Justice & Empowerment.

Introduction of partnership programmes between the old and the young. 100 new day care centres; for older persons were established in collaboration with the Nehru Yuvak Kendra Sangathan. A dialogue was also initiated with school principals to formulate of programme intervention to bring school children and older persons together. As many as 44 now old age homes, 164 new day care centres, 12 new mobile medicare units and one new project for providing non-institutional services to older persons were sanctioned.

An Integrated Programme for Street Children was launched by modifying the existing Schemes for Welfare of Street Children. Child Help Line Telephone Service was launched in as many as 8 cities during the year. An Integrated Programme for Juvenile Justice was launched by modifying the existing Schemes for Prevention and Control of Juvenile Social Maladjustment.

A project to Partnership between the Government - NGO - Corporate Sector was initiated to bring about an improvement in the quality of services provided to children in the homes established under the Juvenile Justice Act, 1986.

The Scheme of Assistance to Voluntary Organisations for providing Social Defence Services was revised. A new performance appraisal system involving Schools of Social Work and reputed NGOs was formulated to carry out assessment of both new as well as ongoing projects. The measure is expected to reduce dependence upon State Governments, cut down delays and ensure better utilisation of funds.

In house training programmes were reintroduced in the NISD.

A Centre for Drug Abuse Prevention has been planned.

A Certificate Training Course on De-addiction Counseling and Rehabilitation' was conducted by the NISD.

A Specially designed Training of Trainers on the addiction counseling Rehabilitation programme was conducted by the NISD for social workers of the North Eastern States.

Central adoption resource agency (CARA)

The Central Adoption Resource Agency has been approved by the Cabinet to register as an Autonomous Body under the Societies Registration Act, 1860. Steps are being taken to register CARA under the said act at the earliest. The Management Committee of the CARA, Ministry of Social Justice and Empowerment has also been constituted vide F.No. 1-6/97-CARA dated 2-11.1998.

Guidelines for uniform Procedure for in-country adoption has been prepared and circulated to the concerned adoption/placement agencies. NCAs/ State Social Welfare Deptts vide D.O. No. 1-4/ -CARA (Pt. 1) dated 14.9.98. Fees payable by adoptive prospective foreign parents have also been enhanced on the recommendation of CARA by Supreme Court of India,

The time, in obtaining the VCA clearance for placing the child in inter-country adoption, has also been reduced from 60 days to 30 days.

The instructions in regard to issue of Passport to the adopted children by foreigners living in a foreign country or by Indian Nationals living abroad or a foreign national of Indian origin living abroad have been issued by Ministry of External Affairs, after consulting the Ministry of Law and Central Adoption Resource Agency.

The shishu Greh Scheme has been revised and the ceiling of Grant in aid has been raised to Rs. 6.00 lakhs per annum in order to facilitate better services for the children.

Norms for financial assistance to VCAs are also under revision.

The Ministry of Finance has approved the creation of 28 posts for the autonomous CARA including one of Secretary CARA at the level of Director to Govt. of India.

Drug abuse prevention

In consonance with the directives of the Prime Minister of India, special focus is given to the drug Abuse Prevention Programme in North East keeping in view the enormity of the problem.

A three day Workshop was conducted on Need Assessment Study of the Problem of drug abuse in North-East at Imphal from 29-31, January, 1997 to assess the ground realities of the problem and plan future interventions. Accordingly, a three pronged strategy has been adopted for the North-East.

(a) Training and enhancing the capabilities of the NGOs in the area.

(b) Extending the outreach of drug abuse prevention scheme of the Ministry By opening of new centres; and

(c) Awareness and Education Programmes for the North-East.

Five Training Programmes for trainers Training Courses for Service Providers in the North East and Attachment training of service providers in reputed Centres is also being implemented. A Committee has been constituted by the Ministry to visit the north Eastern States for reviewing the working of the existing NGOs, explore the possibilities for opening of new Centres and identify service providers for the purpose of training.

The Ministry has established a Centre for Drug Abuse Prevention under the aegis of the National Institute of Social Defence, New Delhi, a subordinate office of the Ministry to serve as the apex body in the country in the field of training, research and documentation in the field of drug abuse prevention. To meet the growing demand of rehabilitation professionals in the country, the Centre has started three months Certificate Course Deaddiction Counselling and Rehabilitation of Drug Abusers from 16 th November, 1998.

Development perspective for the north eastern states

The Ministry organised a two days workshop on "Socio-Economic Development Perspective for the North Eastern States" at Guwahati on 23rd and 24th November, 1998 to discuss the programmes and policies of the Ministry for evolving need based strategies for effective implementation in the North Region.

The workshop was presided over by Minister of State (SJ&E) and attended by Ministers/Ministers incharge of the Eastern States and Sikkim, Senior Officer the Central and State Governments an large number of representatives of Governmental Organisations.

The recommendation of the workshop proved very useful. Consequently, a team of Directors/Deputy Secretaries from each bureau visited the North Eastern States to interact with the concerned State Governments programme implementing agencies to resolve the pending issues and take rem measures for effective implementation of programmes.

4

Scheduled Castes Development

Approximately 13.82 crore people belong to the Scheduled Castes. The concentration of Scheduled Caste population is basically in Uttar Pradesh, West Bengal, Bihar, Tamil Nadu and Andhra Pradesh which account for more than 50% of the SC population. Uttar Pradesh and West Bengal have approximately 20% population belonging to the Scheduled Caste community.

To a large extent, members belonging to the Scheduled Castes mainly earn their livelihood by working on land belonging to land owners or in unclean occupations like scavenging flaying and tanning of leather. More than three quarters of the SC workers are engaged in primary occupations the population of those engaged in the tertiary sector is nearly half the national average. More than 50% of the SC workers are agricultural wage labourers; against the national average of 26%. Though with the spread of urbanisation and governmental measures such as protective legislation and positive discrimination improvements have taken place in the occupational mobility and living standards of the SCs, the majority of them still continue to be worse off than members of other communities. In the field of literacy, as against the national average of 52% the literacy rate of SCs is around 37%. These disparities are further compounded by higher drop out rates in formal education. As a result of all these disadvantages and disparities the proportion of SCs below the poverty line is substantially higher than the national average. Amongst the SCs community itself women are even at a greater disadvantage.

SCP strategy

The vulnerability of the Scheduled Castes severely constrains their access to facilities and programmes of universal coverage. The concept of the Special Component Plan (SCP) was adopted from 1979-80 onwards in recognition of this fact so that there would be a focus on and enhancement of the flow of funds to the Scheduled Castes.

National commission

The National Commission for Scheduled Castes and Scheduled Tribes was constituted under Article 338 of the Constitution to provide a high level independent body to monitor the safeguards provided for scheduled castes and scheduled tribes and also review and report on issues concerning them. The Commission has wide powers and an extensive mandate. The Commission is required to be consulted on major policy matters which effect scheduled castes and scheduled tribes. Like-wise, the National Commission for Safai Karamcharis focuses on the community of safai karamcharis. The National-Commission for Scheduled Castes and Scheduled Tribes has been reconstituted with the following members-

1.	Shri Dilip Singh Bhuria	–Chairperson
2.	Shri Kameswar Paswan	–Vice-Chairperson
3.	Ven Lama Lobzang	–Member
4.	Shri Harinder Khalsa	–Member
5.	Shri Chotray Majhi	–Member
6.	Shri M. Kannan	–Member
9.	Smt, Madhuri Singh	–Member

There are schemes for educational, economic and social development including protective measures under the Protection of Civil Rights Act 1955 and the Scheduled Castes and Scheduled Tribes (Prevention of Atrocities) Act 1989 alongwith the policy of reservation in public employment and education for upliftment of people belonging to scheduled castes. These schemes are implemented through State Governments/Union Territories as Centrally Sponsored Schemes.

Review

Most of the schemes have been revised in the 9th Plan. This has been done to enhance the impact of these schemes and make them more suitable to the needs of the scheduled castes in changing times. The report of the Working Group on Development and Welfare of Scheduled castes during the 9th Plan, submitted in May, 1996, has been taken into account while formulating the Action Plan for the 9th Plan.

Educational development

The scheme of Post-Matric Scholarship for scheduled castes and scheduled tribes has played a major role in last 50 years in assisting SC/ST students to pursue higher education. Around 20 lakh students are provided Scholarship under this scheme each year. In the 9th Plan, changes such as enhancement of maintenance allowance, raising of income-eligibility ceiling and relaxation of restrictions on the number of male children in a family eligible for scholarship were affected. The scheme of Pre-Matric Scholarships is primarily targetted at the children of those scheduled castes who are engaged in unclean occupations such as scavenging. The scheme of National Overseas scholarship for SCs/STs which has been revised now provides financial assistance to those students who pursue higher studies in higher technical -fields abroad. 532 students have benefited under this scheme and have undergone studies in well known universities in Europe, Australia and U.S.A. The scheme for upgradation of Merit of SC/ST students was transferred to the Ministry of Social Justice and Empowerment from the Department of Education, Ministry of Human Resource Development in 1993-94 and was reviewed by all the State. Governments in 1996-97. Under the scheme for Construction of Hostels for SC girls and boys, it was decided to take into account actual costs while computing the central assistance. This scheme is very important as it helps to retain ~SC students in formal education by providing them with boarding and lodging facilities.

Economic development and employment genertion

The National SC/ST Finance and Development Corporation (NSFDC) and the State level SCDCs, to whom the central government provides 49% contribution equity capital, play a major role in the promotion of self employment and income generating activities. The National Safai Karamcharis Finance and Development Corporation (NSKFDC) was also established in 1996-97. The scheme of Coaching and Allied for SCs/STs, provides comprehensive coaching for those candidates who are appearing for various competitive examination to get jobs in government Sector.

Protective measures

The Protection of Civil Rights Act and the SC and (Prevention of Atrocities) Act and Rules are important Central Statutes which are administered a enforced. Central assistance is provided to State Govts. under a Centrally Sponsored Scheme.

Research

This scheme provides funding for evaluation a other research as well as training and awareness workshops. Since 1995-96, in addition to long term studies, several short term studies with a sharp focus on, key schematic issues have been commission through Universities and Governmental as well Non-Governmental institutions. NIRD, IIPA a several voluntary organisations have been funded conduct awareness and training programmes, decision makers, implementers and target groups

Dr. B.R. Ambedkar foundation

Under the aegis of the Ministry, Dr. Baba Saheb Ambedkar Foundation was established in the context of his centenary celebrations to pursue important projects relevant to Dr. Ambedkar's mission such the establishment of a National Library, the institution of University Chairs and award of fellowships advanced studies abroad.

National commission for scheduled castes and scheduled tribes

During 1998, the 30th Report of the erstwhile Commissioner for Scheduled Castes and Schedule Tribes and the First, Second and Special Report the National Commission for Scheduled Castes a Scheduled Tribes alongwith Action Taken Memorandum thereon were laid on the Table of bo Houses of Parliament in July, 1998.

Details of expenditure in scheduled castes development division

During 1996-97, an expenditure of Rs. 708.38 crore was incurred for development of scheduled caste During 1997-98, an amount of Rs. 610.24 crores was spent. Revised estimates for expenditure during 1998-99 is Rs. 735.70 crores.

Special component plan (SCP)

The State/UT wise distribution of the Scheduled Castes in the State/UT having significant population of the SCs is given in the next page. (1991 Census).

Sl. No.	*State/UT*	*% of SC Population to the Total Population of the State/UT*
1.	Andhra Pradesh	15.93
2.	Assam	7.40
3.	Bihar	14.55
4.	Gujarat	7.41
5.	Gujarat	7.41
6.	Haryana	19.75
7.	Himachal Pradesh	25.34
8.	Jammu & Kashmir	8.30
9.	Karnataka	16.38
10.	Kerala	9.92
11.	Madhya Pradesh	14.55
12.	Maharashtra	11.09
13.	Manipur	2.02
14.	Orissa	16.20
15.	Punjab	28.31
16.	Rajasthan	17.29
17.	Sikkim	5.93
18.	Tamil Nadu	19.18
19.	Tripura	16.36
20.	Uttar Pradesh	21.05
21.	West Bengal	23.62
22.	Chandigarh	16.51
23.	Delhi	19.05
24.	Pondicherry	16.25

With the objective of overall development of SCs to bring them above the poverty line and into the mainstream of national life with equal social and economic status with other sections of the population, the strategy of Special Component Plan was evolved in the year 1979. Special Component Plan is designed to channelise the flow of outlays and benefits from the general sectors in the plans of State/UTs and the Central Ministries, at least in proportion to the Scheduled Castes population both in physical and financial terms. It is not a scheme by itself. It is an umbrella under which all schemes implemented by State and Central Governments are dovetailed for addressing different needs of the Scheduled Castes.

Objectives

(1) Direct flow of benefits through family and individual oriented programmes aimed at economic development of the Scheduled Castes, covering major occupational groups like agricultural labourers, small and marginal farmers, primary leather workers (flayers, tanners etc.) rural artisans, fishermen sweepers and scavengers, urban unorganized labourers etc. The objective is to provide income generating assets and skill to enable the SC families to earn sustained income and cross the poverty line.

(2) Provision of drinking water, health services, house sites and housing, drainage, link roads education, vocational guidance etc.

At present 24 State/UTs having sizeable SC population are formulating Special component Plan for the Scheduled Castes.

Flow of funds under SCP

Guidelines have been issued by the Government of India from time to time to the effect that earmarking of funds, for SCP out, of total state- plan outlays should be atleast in proportion to the SC population in the total population of the respective states. The SC population of the country as per 1981 Census was 15.75% of the total population of the country. It has increased to 16.48% in the 1991 census. The SCP outlay was however, only 7.61 % and 8.31 % of the Total State' Plan Outlay in the 6th and 7th five-year plan respectively. The SCP outlay as percentage of total state outlay has increased to 11.03% in the 8th five-year plan as compared to 8.31% in the 7th five-year plan.

Coverage

The details of SC families economically assisted to cross the poverty line, which was monitored under Point 11-A of Twenty Point Programme, during the period 1994-95 to 1997-98 are as under:

Year	*No. of SSC families Economically assisted*
1994-95	26,96,412
1995-96	24,82,075
1996-97	22,98,900
1997-98	20,65,987

The target for 1998-99 is to assist 24.25 lakhs families.

Impact of special component plans on SC population

The percentage of SC population below the poverty line during the last two decades is given below:

Year	*Percentage of SC Population below the poverty line*	
	Rural	*Urban*
1977-78	64.60	54.30
1983-84	53.10	40.40
1993-94	48.11	49.48

It may be seen that the percentage of SC population below the poverty line in the rural areas has come down from 64.60% in 1977-78 to 48.11% in 199394. The same in case of urban areas had shown a dramatic fall from 54.3% in 1977-78 to 40.40% in 1983-84. But in the next decade this figure went up to 49.48 in 1993-94, this may be due to large-scale migration of SC population from the rural to the urban areas.

Action plan for special component plan

It has been observed that even though the State Govt./UT

Administration shave improved their SCP allocations over the years, it has not yet reached to the required minimum level. SCP expenditure in most of the States/ UTs has been quite low during VIII Plan. Since the problems being faced in the SC development continue to be social, economic and educational and the incidence of poverty among SC population is still high, the efforts for the development of SCs need to be accelerated vigorously. Besides increasing the allocation for SCP to the level of percentage of SCs in the States/UTs, strict monitoring to ensure full utilization of funds earmarked under SCP and effective implementation of schemes under SCP of various development departments has become quite essential. The following suggestions have been issued to the State Governments/UT Administrations in connection with the formulation and implementation of SCP:

(i) Earmarking of funds of SCP from Total State Plan outlay, at least, in proportion of SC population in the total population of the State/ LIT.

(ii) Making the Social Welfare Department/or the department concerned with the SC welfare and development of SCs as nodal department for formulation and implementation of SCP.

(iii) Placing the funds earmarked for SCP at the disposal of the nodal department concerned with the SC welfare and development, which in turn will re-allocate the funds to the sectional departments for implementing schemes directly relevant to SC development.

(iv) Placing the funds earmarked the SCP under separate budget head/sub-hear for each development department implementing SCP.

(v) To constitute State and District/Block level Monitoring Committees to monitor the implementation of various schemes under SCP of various development department. The District/ Block level Committees may review the progress of implementation of schemes and utilization of funds on monthly basis and the State level Committee may review the progress on quarterly basis.

(vi) Members of parliament State Legislative Assembly in the concerned Zilla Parishad/ Block Panchayat area, prominent SC personnel/social worker who are well acquinted with the problems of SCs, representative of NGOs working for the welfare of SCs and SC members of village Panchayats may also be included in the State/ District/Block level Monitoring Committees.

(vii) The District/Block level Monitoring Committees may be made responsible for identifying the developmental needs of SCs living in various Panchayat areas falling under the jurisdiction of concerned District/Block and suggest suitable schemes for their developments. This process may be completed by the end of the third quarter of the financial year and reported to the nodal department concerned with SC welfare and development which will in consultation with concerned development departments may formulate suitable schemes with financial and physical targets for implementation during the next financial year.

(viii) The nodal department may ensure timely release of funds to the concerned development departments and the development departments may ensure immediate release of funds soon after the receipt of funds from nodal department, to their field level implementing agencies. Any lapse on the part of field level implementing agencies in timely utilisation of funds and proper implementation of the schemes may be viewed seriously.

(ix) Evaluation of assess the impact of economic development schemes implemented under SCP, on the socio-economic conditions of SCs may be got conducted by the nodal department on regular basis. Dissemination of information to SCs all over the State/UT about the schemes/programmes available for their development may be the responsibility of the nodal department. The nodal department may also ensure the follow up of - the schemes implemented and maintenance of proper records on assets Districts/Blocks etc.

Special compnent plan of central ministries

The strategy of special component plan at the central Govt. level involve participation of central government ministries/departments in formulating specific plans for the scheduled castes under Annual Plans of respective Ministries/Departments. Many Central Ministries cater to the areas of vital importance to the SCs. The SCP at the central government level as a crucial role to play in the development of SCs.

The ministry of Social Justice and Empowerment has maintained close liasion with Central Ministries Departments and impressed upon them the need to the formulate and implement comprehensive Special Component Plan. The Ministries have also been requested to open separate Budget Head/Sub He, for Special Component Plan.

Special central assistanceto special component plan for scheduled caste

The main objective of the Special Central Assistance to Special Component Plan for Scheduled Castes to give a thrust to the development programmes for scheduled castes with reference to their occupation pattern and the need for increasing their productivity and income from their limited resources. It would help in bringing about occupational diversification i the labour surplus economy. Further the SCA is expected to fill the gaps which various central an state development programmes are not in a position to fill. It was realised that the programmes for which the SCA could be used by the State Governments would vary from state to state and region to region within the same sate depending on the local occupational patterns and the economic activities, available. Even within the same state and region they would vary from time to time.

As an additive to the state's plan and programmes, the Special Central Assistance is expected to be an effective instrument in catalysing and strengthening the Special Component Plans as a whole in each state. The quantum of Special Central Assistance is related to the special component plans of the States/ UTs especially in concrete terms such as number of scheduled castes families that will cross the poverty Line by the programmes and outlays in each sector, and the optimality of the state special component plan in comparison with the scheduled caste population in the state. The performance of the states in implementation of the programmes for the scheduled castes is also taken into account.

The Central scheme of Special Central Assistance (SCA) to Special Component Plan of States/UTs is linked to Government of India's strategy for the socio-economic development of the scheduled castes. It is an additive to the Special Component Plan (SCP) of the states/UTs and is intended for augmenting the totality of States efforts for the economic development of SCs. The underlying objective of the SCA which is a central grant to the States/UTs is that it should be used to give an added thrust to the development programme for SCs with reference to their occupational needs for increasing the productivity of and income from their limited assets by taking up family oriented schemes for them. It is used to fill the critical gaps and provide the central government a leverage in directing flow of funds in areas critical -to the development needs of the SCs.

The scheme was started in 1979-80 with a token provision of Rs. 5.00 crores. It has evolved as an alternative instrument at the disposal of Government of India to bring about qualitative change in the living conditions of the SCs and among more vulnerable groups of SCs (such as scavengers, flayers and tanners). In order to provide greater scope for effectiveness of SCA in achieving government's objective, the existing guidelines on SCA have been amplified in the year 1993. The amplified guidelines stipulate that states/UTs can utilise the SCA for infrastructural development programmes in blocks having 50% or more of Scheduled Castes population subject to the condition that the SCA allocation should be made use of in a such a way as to encourage 'larger efforts on the development of SCs on the part of the States/UTs.

The condition of blocks having 50% or more of SO population for use of SCA for infrastructural development programmes has been relaxed and villages having 50% or more of SO population can now be considered for infrastructural development programmes with the support of SCA funds. Only 10% of the total SCA released to the state government/UT Administration in a year should be utilised for infrastructural development programmes. According to the amplified guidelines, SCA to SOP can be used for various development sectors on specific viable schemes covering Scheduled Castes population individually and/or in clusters.

Utilisation of SCA

States/UTs have been given full flexibility in utilising SCA subject to the condition that it should be used in conjunction with SOP on family oriented income generating economic development programmes/ schemes and for infrastructural development programmes in the villages having 50% or more of SC population.

(1) 15% of the total SCA released to the States/UTs, on the basis of the criteria mentioned below will be utilised by the State Government/UT Administrations exclusively on viable income-generating economic development schemes/ programmes for SO Women.

(2) 5% of the total SCA released to the States/UTs will be utilised by them exclusively for the economic development of disabled persons among SCs.

(3) 3% of the total SCA released to the States/UTs will be utilised by the States/UTs for supervision, monitoring and evaluation of economic development schemes implemented with the support of SCA funds.

Criteria for the release of SCA

SCA is released to the States/UTs implementing SCP on the following criteria:—

1. (a) on the basis of SO population of the State/UT 40%

   (b)on the basis of relative backwardness of the State/UT 10%

2. (a) on the basis of percentage of SO families in the State/UT covered by composite economic development programmes in the State/UT Plan to enable them to cross the poverty line 25%

(b) on the basis of percentage of SOP to the Annual Plan as compared to SO population percentage in the state/UTs. 25%

Second instalment of SCA should be released to the States/UTs after ensuring expenditure of cumulative opening balances of the previous year and 75% of the first instalment for the current year.

2% of the total budget allocation for the scheme will be earmarked for North Eastern States which implement SOP of SCs.

Disbursement of SCA

The amount of SCA released by the Government of India and utilised by the States/UTs for the period 1994-95 to 1998-99 is given below:

(Rs. in lakhs)

Period	*Released*	*Utilised*	*% Utilised*
Sixth Five Year Plan	60,000.00	56810.94	94.68
Seventh Five Year Plan	87,600.00	86191.58	98.39
Eighth Five Year Plan	134,476.96	135,058.20	100.43
1997-98	308,27.00	31096.57	100.87
1998-99	218,62,96.00	11308.96	51.72
		(upto Sept. 98)	

State/UT wise details of release and utilisation of SCA to SOP for the year 1994-95 to 1998-99 are given in the Annexure II.

During the financial year 1998-99, an amount of Rs. 361.00 crore has been allocated and out of which Rs. 218.63 crores have already been released to the States/ UTs till now.

Performance

The utilisation of SCA is monitored through quarterly/ annual progress report from the State Governments/ UT Administrations. The details of utilisation of SCA during the VIII Plan period and during 1997-98 have been examined and it is observed that the utilisation has been satisfactory. In fact over the years, SCA has become a powerful instrument for the poverty alleviation programmes for SCs. However, in a few cases shortcomings were noticed. There is undue delay by the State/UTs in releasing funds to the implementing agencies which results in funds lying unspent at the end of financial year. Late release of funds to the implementing agencies/ departments non-utilisation of funds sanctioned/ released to the implementing agencies/departments to the implementing agencies/ departments for the purpose for which it is sanctioned, accumulation of unspent balance of funds for considerable long period with the implementing agencies/department keeping funds in Civil Deposits, Fixed Deposits, Saving Bank Accounts, P.L.A. etc. for considerable long period, lack of proper action plan for implementation of schemes, sanction of funds for schemes without ascertaining their feasibility and viability, leakage of benefit of schemes meant for SCs to Non-SCs, etc. decelerate the process of economic development of the target group. An effective device needs to be evolved to remove such shortcomings/ loopholes so that the purpose of SCA could be served meaningfully. Amongst various measure for effective implementation of development schemes for SCs, the following points may be given more stress.- The Government of India have suggested the following points for effective implementation of the programmes:–

i) Release of funds to the implementing agencies without loss of time after getting the SCA from the Government of India.

ii) Seperate account of SCA released to the implementing agencies may be maintained and utilisation of SCA funds by the implementing agencies may be watched regularly through periodical progress reports from the implementing agencies.

iii) It may be ensured the Utilisation Certificates from the concerned implementing agencies are obtained in time.

iv) Annual Audit of SCA Accounts of State and District/Block level implementing agencies may be ensured.

v) Keeping SCA funds in civil deposits, fixed deposits, saving Bank accounts, PLA etc. for long periods by implementing agencies or nodal department may be discouraged. Release of funds to the implementing agencies without ascertaining the utilisation of funds released to them earlier leads to accumulation of unspent balances and increase in the deposit in various accounts. Identification of viable schemes as per the developmental needs of SCs and identification of eligible beneficiaries to be considered assistance in a financial year should completed well before the commencement the financial year. Sanction of schemes , release of assistance can thus be ensured time soon after the receipt of SCA funds. This will help in avoiding last minute sanction schemes at the fag end of the financial year and in ensuring full utilisation of funds.

Assistance to scheduled castes development corporations (SCDCs)

In march, 1979, the Centre initiated a Centra sponsored scheme of assistance to State Governments for participating in the share equity the Scheduled Castes

Development Corporation (SCDCs) in the ratio of 49:51. At present, SCDCs are functioning in 25 States/UTs which includes SCDCs which are common to SCs and STs.

Functions of SCDCs

(i) Identification of eligible SC/ST families and motivating them to undertake economic development schemes.

(ii) Sponsoring the schemes to financial, institutions for credit support.

(iii) Providing financial assistance in the form c margin money at low rate of interest an subsidy in order to reduce the repayment liability.

(iv) Providing necessary tie up with other proverb alleviation programmes.

Implementation of the schemes

The SCDCs have been acting as guarantors and promoters for credit support and providing missing inputs by way of margin money loans and subsidy to the target group. They have a useful role in the mobilisation for fiances for economic development of scheduled castes living below the poverty line. The SCDCs mainly take up employment oriented schemes in the following areas-

(i) Agriculture and allied including minor Irrigation.

(ii) Small Scale Industry.

(iii) Transport

(iv) Trade and Service Sector

Performance

Project assistance from banks is arranged by SCDCs besides providing margin Assistance out of share capital assistance and subsidy out of Special Central Assistance (SCA) funds. The SCDCs are experiencing difficulties in arranging bank finances. The share from banks is unduly delayed or highly inadequate. Besides, there are other structural, organisational and managerial factors which hamper the activities of the SCDCs. The beneficiaries covered so far under scheme are as under:—

Year	*No. of beneficiaries (in lakh)*
1980-85	28.69
1985-90	29.22
1990-91	5.42
1991-92	4.52
1992-93	5.35
1993-94	5.32
1994-95	6.31
1995-96	4.20
1996-97	4.61
1997-98	3.71

Budgetary support

Plan outlay and expenditure details of Central share capital assistance to SCDCs are given below:—

(Rs. in Crores)

Year	*Plan outlay*	*Expenditure*
1992-93	20.00	22.07
1993-94	22.00	29.34
1994-95	22.00	22.00
1995-96	30.00	31.00
1996-97	30.00	31.99
1997-98	45.00	45.00
1998-99 (30.11.98)	60.00	35.85

Modification in the scheme

In order to streamline the criteria of release of Central Share Equity to SCDCs, following conditions have been laid for release of Central funds to them w.e.f. current year–

(i) Minimum recovery rate of the loans disbursed should be 60% in a financial year.

(ii) Minimum utilisation of Central Share should be 75% in a financial year.

(iii) Prior release of State Share to SCDC.

(iv) Ability of the SCDCs to raise additional resource from financial institutional including banks.

National scheduled castes and scheduled tribes finance and development corporation (NSFDC)

The National Scheduled Castes and Scheduled Tribes Finance and Development Corporation (NSFDC) was established on 8th February, 1989 as a Government Company not for profit under Section 25 of the Companies Act, 1956. The focus of NSFDC is on the special developmental and financing needs (loans only) of the SCs and STs over the above the credit available through priority sector lending of banks and other institutions. The authorised share capital of NSFDC has been enhanced from Rs. 300 crores to Rs. 1000 crores during the current financial year. The paid up capital of this Corporation is Rs. 342.43 crores.

NSFDC provides financial assistance at concessional rates for income generating activities and training in skill development to SCs and STs whose annual income is below double the poverty line criteria i.e. Rs. 22,000 per annurn in rural areas and Rs. 23,700 per annum in urban areas. The assistance is provided through the various States Scheduled Castes Development Corporations (SCDCs) and other State Channelising Agencies (SCAs) for implementing technically feasible and financially viable schemes/projects besides providing grants for skill development programmes organised by SCAs and Non-Govern mental Organisations (NGOs).

Implementation of schemes

The Corporation provides term loans, seed capital, bridge loans etc. at concessional rates of interest. A maximum loan of 85% of the project cost is provided. With the revision of the financing pattern w.e.f. 1-10-95, projects upto Rs. 30 lakhs, can be, financed by the Corporation. NSFDC finances schemes in the following sectors:-

(i) Agriculture and Allied
(ii) Horticulture
(iii) Animal Husbandry and dairying
(iv) Minor Irrigation
(v) Small Industries
(vi) Trade Services and
(vii) Transport etc.

Performance

NSFDC's performance has gained momentum over the years. Disbursements have risen substantially from Rs. 35 lakhs in 1989-96 to Rs. 486.57 crores (cumulative) as on 30th November, 1998. The details of disbursements -are as under-

Recovery

The recovery position of NSFDC from its channelising agencies is around 87.67%. However, recovery from the beneficiaries is reported to much lower.

National scheme of liberation and rehabilitation of scavengers and their dependents (NSLRS)

The National Scheme of Liberation and Rehabilitation of Scavengers and their dependents was launched by the

Government of India in March, 1992, in pursuance of the commitment to eliminate the inhuman practice of manual handling of might soil and filth by the end of VIII Plan period, with the following three components.

(i) a period survey to identify scavengers and their dependents and their aptitude for alternative trades and professions,

(ii) training of scavengers and their dependents and

(iii) rehabilitation of scavengers through projects with a prescribed funding pattern.

(Rs. in Crores)

Year	*Amount*
1989-90	0.35
1990-91	6.22
1991-92	40.50
1992-93	43.93
1993-94	32.21
1994-95	77.59
1995-96	90.11
1996-97	71.47
1997-98	93.89
1998-99	30.26
(30th November, 1998)	

The Corporation has so far sanctioned 1490 projects, which on completion would benefit around 218497 beneficiaries.

Implementing agencies

The implementation of the Scheme at the grass level is looked after by the SCAs/SCDCs. National Safai Karamcharis Finance Development Corporation (NSKFDC) has entrusted with the responsibility of day-today implementation and monitoring of the scheme as well as coordination and collaboration with the SCDCs implementing the scheme. The 0 implementation of the scheme has been entrusted to the District Collectors/ Deputy Commissioners Training is imparted through existing institutes Central Govt., State Govts., Semi Government and Non-government-organisations.

Financial assistance

Training

The scavengers are imparted training in such trades of their aptitude which can successfully provide them alternative placement. The training cost is borne by the Government of India and during the course of training, the trainee gets stipend upto Rs. 500/- per month, besides honorarium to trainer upto Rs. 300/- per month and tool kit allowance upto Rs. 800/-; as per the TRYSEM norms.

National safai Karmacharis finance and development corporation (NSKFDC)

The Government approved the setting up of the National Safai Karamcharis Finance and Development Corporation (NSKFDC) under Section 25 of the Companies Act, 1956 with its registered office at Delhi, with an authorised share capital Rs. 200 crores.

The NSKFDC has been incorporated on 24-01-1997. The paid up share capital of the Corporation is Rs. 14.75 crores. The major objectives for setting up a separate Financial Corporation for Safai Karamcharis are to promote economic development/self employment for the economic rehablitation of safai karmacharis besides providing training in technical and entrepreneurial skills and extending loans to students from safai karamchari community for pursuing higher education.

The NSKFDC will function as an apex institution for channelising funds through the State Chennelising Agencies authorised by the State Governments/UT Administrations.

The NSKFDC will also coordinated and monitor the scheme programmes implemented through authorised State Finance and Development Corporations/Boards/UT Administrations financed by the Corporation.

The Corporation had started its operations by the last quarter of 1997 and during 1997-98 the Corporation disbursed Rs. 384.39 lakhs for 14 schemes to its various channelising agencies benefitting 459 safai karamcharis.

A budgetary provision of Rs. 10 crores was made for this Corporation during the current financial year which has since been released to them. Upto December 1998 the Corporation sanctioned 29 projects benefitting 2320 safai karamcharis.

Rehabilitation

There is a prescribed financial package for rehabilitation of scavengers in alternative trades through provision of financial assistance upto Rs. 50,000/- per beneficiary.

This includes a subsidy of 50% of the capital cost subject to a ceiling of 10,000/- per project, margin money loan of 15% of the project cost at 4% rate of interest, and the remaining portion by way of loan finance to be provided by commercial banks.

The Govt. of India have released Rs. 525.16 crores to the State during the period 1991-92 to 1997-998, for implementation of the Scheme. The year-wise details alongwith physical progress are indicated in the next page.

Year	Funds released to State GGovts. (Rs. in crore)	No. of Scavengers	
		Trained	Rehabilitated
(1)	(2)	(3)	(4)
1991-92	50.50	–	–
1992-93	60.73	16220	18411
1993-94	70.97	22241	41160
1994-95	73.00	25272	62269
1995-96	91.96	26493	80016
1996-97	90.00	21779	60565
1997-98	90.00	15359	27887

The Scheme was last modified w.e.f. 1.4.1996 to bring further improvements in its implementation. The important modifications done are mentioned below:–

(i) Release of Central Assistance to Scheduled Castes Development Corporations directly.

(ii) Adoption of TRYSEM norms for training.

(iii) Higher project cost of Rs. 50,000/- per beneficiary, for rehabilitation.

(iv) Cluster approach for training & rehabilitation.

Centrally sponsored scheme of post matric scholarship to students belonging to SCs and STs

Objectives

The Scheme provides financial assistance to such students belonging to SCs and STs who pursue recognised post matriculation courses in recognised institutions, including correspondence courses, within the country.

Elements of scholarship

The financial assistance includes provision of maintenance allowance, reimbursement of compulsory non-refundable fees, thesis typing/ printing charges, study tour charges, book allowance for students pursuing correspondence courses and special provisions for such students with disabilities who are covered under the scheme.

Implementing agency and funding pattern

The Scheme is implemented by the respective State Governments and Union Territory Administrations receive 100% central assistance from Government of India over and above their respective Committed Liability, which is borne by them. The Committed Liability of North Eastern States has, however, been dispensed with from commencement of Ninth FiveYear Plan period.

Performance

The Scheme which was introduced in the year 1944 with a coverage of 114 students, has picked up very well over the years and is at present covering over 20 lakhs students. The Following table shows the performance of the scheme during Eighth Five-Year Plan period.

Year cation (Rs. in crores)	*Budget allo- assistance released (Rs. in crores)*	*Central beneficiaries*	*No. of*
1994-95	96.35	96.35	1,42,656
1995-96	145.00	144.86	17,90,355
1996-97	149.00	179.93	17,12,420
1997-98	54.17 (R.E.)	54.17	17,21,994
1998-99	100.00 (R.E.)	99.86	20,99,159
		(Upto Dec '98)	(Anticipated)

Modifications done

It has been decided to continue the scheme during the

Ninth Five Year Plan period also with following modifications:—

(1) Income ceilings

The following table shows the pre-revised and revised income ceiling w.e.f. 1.4.98.

Income ceiling limits of Parents Revised:

Pre-revised	Revised	Scholarship eligibility towards maintenance allowance
Rs. 33,400	Rs. 38,220	Full maintenance allowance, full fees.
Rs. 44,500	Rs. 50,920	(I) Full maintenance allowance and fees in Group A. (II) Half maintenance allowance and full fees for courses in Group B, C, D and E.

The revised income ceilings account-for consumer price index for industrial workers upto Oct, 1997.

(II) Removal of restrictive clause

Prior to modifications in the scheme, only two male children of the same parents/guardians were eligible to get the benefits under the scheme and there was no such restriction in case of female children. In the modified scheme, the restrictive clause has been totally removed w.e.f . 1.4.98 and now all children of the same parents/ guardians are eligible to get the benefits of the scheme, if otherwise eligible.

(III) Dispensation of committed liability of north eastern states

The funding pattern of the scheme is such that 100% central assistance is provided to State/UTs implementing the scheme, over and above their respective Committed

Liability, which is equal to the expenditure reached during the terminal year of the last Five Year Plan period and this level of expenditure is required to be borne by them. The North Eastern States were not in a position to provide for the Committeed Liability in their State resources, owing to their severe financial constraints arising out of substantial expenditure required to be incurred by them on maintenance of law and order for containing insurgency etc.

As a consequence, the North Eastern States could not receive any central assistance during 1997-98 and resultantly a large number of students could not get benefits of the scheme. The Government is since committed towards accelerating the development of North Eastern States, therefore, it has been decided to dispense with the Committed Liability of the North Eastern States from the commencement of Ninth Five Year Plan period. This has eased the financial burden of North Eastern States to an extent of Rs. 20.83 crores per year, thus benefiting around 2 lakhs students, every year. As a consequence of the dispensation of Committed Liability, central assistance of Rs. 32.61 crores has already been released to the North Eastern States during 1998-99 (upto December, 1998).

(IV) Additional provisions for SC and ST students with disabilities

Keeping in view the provisions of the Persons with Disabilities (Equal Opportunities Protection of Rights and Full Participation) Act 1995 the following additional provisions for students with disabilities have been introduced in the Scheme w.e.f. 1.4.98. The disability as per the Act is defined as blindness, low vision, leprosy-cured, hearing impairment, locomotor disability, mental retardation and mental illness.

Timely sanction/disbursements

Sanction and disbursement of scholarship by States/UTs involves a large number of students and a multiplicity of levels. The Ministry in this regard have circulated to all States/UTs. on 4.4.95, the detailed guidelines for streamlining sanction and disbursement procedures under the Scheme.

Centrally sponsored scheme of pre matric scholarship to the children of those engaged in unclean occupations

Objectives

The Scheme financially assists the children of scavengers, sweepers having traditional link with scavenging, flayers and tanners, irrespective of their religion, to pursue education upto matriculation level.

Implementing agency and funding pattern

The Scheme is implemented by the State Governments and Union Territory Administration. Central assistance is provided to the State Government on 50:50 basis and 100% to Union Territory Administration over and above their Committed Liability.

Elements of scholarship

The Scheme covers day scholars from class I to X with scholarship rates from Rs. 25 per month for classes I to V, Rs. 40 per month for classes VI to X and Rs. 50 per month for classes IX and X. The scheme also covers hostellers from classes III to X. The scholarship rate for hostellers in classes III to VIII is Rs. 200 per month and is Rs. 250 per month-for classes IX and X The scholarship is provided for 10 months in a year. Besides scholarship, an adhoc grant of Rs. 500 per annum is also provided to day schoalrs as well as hostellers. The additional provisions for students amongst target groups with disabilities have also been introduced w.e.f. 1.4.98, keeping in view the provisions of the Persons with Disabilities (Equal Opportunities, Protection of Right, and Full Participation) Act, 1995.

Performance

It has been decided to continue the scheme during the Ninth Five-year Plan period also. There is no income ceiling prescribed under the scheme. Upto two children of the same parents/guardians can get the benefits of the scheme, if pursuing classes IX and X. For pursuing classes upto class VIII, though there is no such resctriction, however, if a 3rd or subsequent child is borne after 1.4.93, then only upto two children of the same parents can get benefits of the scheme.

The scheme was initially introduced in the year 1978 and over the year the scheme has picked up and the present likely coverage of beneficiaries is over 3 lakhs. The following table gives the performance of the scheme since 1994-95:-

(Rs. in crores)

Year	*Budget Alocation Released*	*Central Assistance (in lakhs)*	*No. of Beneficiaries*
1994-95	10.00	6.25	1.76
1995-96	7.50	8.92	2.83
1996-97	7.50	14.04	3.00
1997-98	2.00	2.00	3.62
1998-99	4.00	3.95 (upto Dec '98)	4.09 (Anticipated)

The State/UT wise coverage of beneficiaries and central assistance released since 1997-98.

National overseas scholarship scheme for SC, ST etc. students for higher studies bbroad

Objectives

The Scheme provides financial assistance to meritorious selected students for pursuing higher studies abroad in specified fields of Masters level courses, Ph.D and Post - Doctoral research programmes in Engineering, Technology and Science only.

Brief description

It has been decided to revive the Scheme w.e.f. 1998-99 to 2000-2001, with modifications. The regulations governing the scheme are accordingly being finalised. The modified scheme when finalised would provide enhanced maintenance allowance of US $77001- per annum or Pounds Sterling 5000/- per annum for candidates in U.K., for all levels of courses covered under the scheme. Prior to modifications, the maintenance allowance varied from US $59404 per annum to US $77004 per annum, depending upon the levels of the courses.

The contingency allowance for books, essential apparatus, study tour charges, typing and binding of thesis etc., has also been raised from US $3854 to US $5004 per annum or Pound Sterling 325/- per annum, for candidates in U.K. The modified scheme would also provide reimbursement of actual visa fees in Indian rupees.

The scheme also provides air passage by the shortest route and by economy class, by arrangements with the national carrier, poll tax, equipment allowance and incidental journey expenses, actual fees charged by the institution and the medical insurance premia. The awardees are also permitted to supplement their prescribed allowance by undertaking research/teaching assistantship upto US $2400/- per annum or Pounds

Sterling 1560/- per annum, for candidates in U.K. and beyond these ceilings, the maintenance allowance will be proportionately reduced. The financial assistance under the scheme is available to the finally selected students sent abroad, for the maximum period of 4 years for Ph.D. research, for 3 years for Master's Programme and for 1 and 112 year for Post Doctoral research. The income of the awardees if employed, or of their parents/guardians, should not exceed Rs. 12000/- per month. Not more than one child of the same parents/guardians is eligible to get benefits of the scheme and the awardee can get only one time benefit under the scheme. The prospective awardee should not be more than 35 years of the age as on the first day of the month of the advertisement of the scheme. The scheme provides for 30 awardees per year, out of which 17 are for SCs, 9 are for STs, 1 is for Denotified, Nomadic and Semi-nomadic Tribes, 2 are for SCs converts to other religion and 1 is for landless agricultural labourers and traditional artisans.

Performance

The scheme was introduced in 1954-55 and since then a total, of 732 awards have been offered, out of which 532 awards have been availed of budget allocations and the expenditure incurred under this non-plan Scheme since 1994-95 is given below:-

(Rs. in lakhs)

Year	*Budget Allocation*	*Expenditure*
1994-95	562.00	562.00
1995-96	490.00	390.81
1996-97	490.00	180.00
1997-98	490.00	226.00
1998-99	390.00	80.60 (Upto Dec'98)

Nine passage grants in a year to Scheduled Castes (4 grants), Scheduled Tribes (4 grants) and Denotified, Nomadic and Semi-Nomadic Tribes (one grant) are also provided, which are open throughout the year.

Only those candidates who are in receipt of a merit scholarship for Post Graduate- Studies, Research or Training abroad (excluding attending seminars, workshops, conferences), from a foreign government/ organisation or under any other scheme, where the cost of passage is not provided, are eligible.

The candidates should possess a Master's or an equivalent degree in Technical, Engineering and Science disciplines. The candidates who have already reached abroad, are not considered for passage grants.

The eligibility conditions otherwise are same as under the Scheme of National Overseas Scholarship for SC, ST etc. candidates. The air passage is provided by economy class and by shortest route through arrangements with the national carrier.

Central sector scheme of special educational development programme for scheduled sastes girls belonging to very low literacy level

Objectives

The Scheme was introduced during 1996-97 on pilot basis with an objective to provide a package of educational inputs through residential schools for SC girls in areas of very low SC female literacy where traditions and environment are not conducive to their learning.

The schools are intended to supplement the existing measures to impart and consolidate literacy and to promote quality education to such girls who are first generation learners in areas of low literacy.

Elements of the scheme

The school premises consist of classrooms, hostels, kitchens and staff quarters.

The schools function from the suitable hired premises. Grant-in-aid under the scheme comprises the package of Rs. 11,340/- per student in class I only, which includes direct facilities to the students as well as cost towards infrastructure, staff and other running cost. No fees, charges or contributions are charged from the students.

Implementing agency

The Scheme is implemented by the Zila Parishads (District Level Panchayats) of the concerned district. The Zila Parishads may run the schools themselves or through credible NGOs of proven integrity, competence and experience.

The grant is given directly to concerned Zila Parishads, which are required to send their proposals to the Ministry through their State Governments.

Selection of districts

As per 1981 census, 48 districts situated in Bihar, Madhya Pradesh, Rajasthan and Uttar Pradesh have been identified where the literacy of SC girls is less than 2%. The scheme accordingly covers only such districts.

Performance

The Scheme was introduced on pilot basis in the year 1996-97. As against the target of 21 residential schools in the year 1996-97, 20 residential schools were sanctioned to Zila Parishads in Bihar, Madhya Pradesh, Rajasthan and Uttar Pradesh with grant-in-aid of Rs. 34 lakhs, out of the total budget provision of Rs. 60 lakhs for the year.

The performance of the scheme since 1996-97, is given below:–

Year	*Budget Allocation (Rs. in lakhs)*	*Grant-in-aid released (Rs. in lakhs)*	*No. of schools funded*
1996-97	60.00	34.00	20
1997-98	15.00 (R.E.)	11.75	7
1998-99	150.00 (R.E.)	4.62 (upto Dec '98)	3

Centrally sponsored scheme of girls hostels for scheduled castes

The main objective of the Scheme of Hostels for cheduled Castes is to provide hostel facilities to Scheduled Caste students studying in middle school, higher secondary school, colleges and universities. Under this scheme, financial assistance is provided to the State Governments on 50:50 matching share basis 11,00% to UTs for the construction of boundary walls, two room set for hostel warden and one room set for chowkidar. A Sew rooms/ blocks of the hostels should be constructed barrier free and facilities like ramps etc. should be incorporated in the design of their construction so as to enable the disabled SC student to reside in them coveniently. The cost of construction of hostels is worked out on the basis of State/CPWD schedule of rates. The releases out of the allocated Central share and number of covered inmates is as follows:-

(Rs. in Crores)

Year	*Allocation (CA)*	*Release sanctioned*	*Hostels seats*	*No. of*
1994-95	6.20	6.20	73	7,208
1995-96	7.00	5.65	90	7,546
1996-97	7.00	6.48	37	1,441
1997-98	8.00	6.00	78	12,851
Total	28.20	18.33	278	29,046

During the year 1998-99 against the Budget allocation of Rs. 8.00 Crores an amount of Rs. 4.61 has been released upto Dec., 1998 to the States/UT's.

The Scheme has been revised w.e.f. the financial year 1998-99. The salient feature of the revised scheme are:-

1. Financial Assistance is given for construction of SC/ST hostels to the State Governments on 50:50 basis.
2. 100% grant to Union Territories.
3. 90% grant to Centrally Controlled Universities.
4. In case of other Universities the share of Central Government will be 45% that of concerned State Government will be 45% and the University will contribute 10% towards total cost. However in case the concerned State Government is not able to contribute its expected share of 45%, the University may bear the share of former also thereby bringing up its net contribution to 55%.
5. Land for construction of hostel has to be provided by the State Government, Union Territory and Universities.
6. NGOs are given Central Assistance for expansion of existing hostels on 45 Central share, 45% State share and 10% by the NGO themselves.
7. Universities are also funded on the same basis as NGOs.
8. A few rooms blocks of the hostels should be constructed barrier free to enable the disabled SC student to reside in them conveniently.
9. In order to integrate the SC students with the mainstream accommodation of 10% non-SC students in such hostels should be compulsory. However, if after accommodating all applicant SC candidates

first, certain teats are left vacant, then accommodating to the non-SC students may be considered.

Centrally sponsored scheme of boys hostels for scheduled castes

The Scheme started from the year 1989-90 is implemented on the same pattern as that of Girls Hostels described earlier. The outlay under is Scheme is as under:

(Rs. in Crores)

Year	*Allocation (CA)*	*Release sanctioned*	*Hostels seats*	*No. of*
1994-95	6.20	10.00	327	24,071
1995-96	10.00	14.83	134	11,297
1996-97	10.00	9.40	90	3,580
1997-98	11.00	9.05	27	282
Total	37.20	43.28	578	39,230

During the year 1998-99 against the allocation of Rs. 11.00 crores an amount of Rs. 5.75 crores has been released upto Dec., 1998 to State/UT's.

Book banks for scheduled castes & scheduled tribes

The Scheme is intended to provide SC/ST students access to the latest text books for Medical (including Indian systems of medicine and Homoepathy), veterinary,—Engineering, Agriculture and Polytechnic courses, which require expensive books, through the establishment of book banks.

The scheme also includes Law Courses, Chartered Accountancy, MBA and Bio-Sciences. Each set of books is shared by two students at various stages except in respect of Post-Graduate courses and Chartered Accountancy where it will be one set for each student and the scheme is open to all those in receipt of post-matric scholarships.

The life period of one set of book has been fixed for 3 years. The scheme also provides upto Rs. 2,000/- for purchase of cup-boards.

The ceiling cost per set of text books varies from Rs. 2,400/- to Rs-. 7,500/- depending on the course. Central Assistance is provided to the states on 50% basis (100% to UT's.)

A.	Degree Course (1 set for 2 students)	Cost of one set
1.	Medical	Rs. 7,500.00
2.	Engineering	Rs. 7,500.00
3.	Veterinary	Rs. 5,000.00
4.	Agriculture	Rs. 4,500.00
5.	Polytechnics	Rs. 2,400.00
B.	Post-Graduate Course	
1.	Post Graduate courses in Medical Engg., Agriculture and Veterinary Courses and such other technical/ alike Courses as are approved by the Universities/Institutes of Higher Learning	Rs.5,000.00 (1 set per student)
		(Contd..)
2.	Law Courses L.L.B (3 years and 5 years L.L.B. (2 years)	Rs. 5,000.00 (1 set per student)
3.	Chartered Accountancy (Inter-mediate and Final)	Rs 5,000 00 (1 set per student)
4.	M.B.A (2 years) and similar courses	Rs 5,000.00 (1 set per student)
5.	Bio-Sciences	Rs.5,000.00 (1 set per student)

The expenditure/re leases out of the Central share and number of SC/ST students benefited under the Scheme is as given in the next page.

(Rs. in Crores)

Year	Allocation	Releases students	No. of SC/ST
1994-95	3.50	2.96	37,877
1995-96	3.60	2.64	26,567
1996-97	3.60	1.83	18,927
1997-98	3.60	1.50	16,482

During the year 1998-99 against the allocation of Rs. 3.60 crores an amount of Rs. 0.25 crores has been released upto Dec., 1998 to State/U.T's.

Centrally sponsored coaching & allied scheme for SC/ST students

Under this scheme free coaching facilities are provide to SC/ST, candidates through Pre Examination Training Centres to enable them to compete successfully in the competitive examination conducted by UPSC, SSC, Railway Board, from the financial year 1998-99. Under the revised scheme Post Graduate level courses including Law, Chartered Accountancy, MBA have been included. Provision has also been made to include Brailley Books to help the visually handicapped students also to avail benefit of this Scheme.

Central assistance to States/UT's for setting up of Book Banks is limited to the following ceilling or actual cost of a set, whichever is less:–

Commissions, Public Undertakings and various other recruiting bodies with a view to improving the representation of SCs/STs in various services and posts under Central/State Governments and Public Undertakings etc. This Scheme has been revised for implementation during IXth Plan period. Under the revised scheme Central Assistance is provided on per unit cost basis. Universities and Private Institutes are funded 100% on contractual basis while State owned PETCs will be funded 50% of the contractual amount. There will be no committed liability of the State Government. The grant is released in two equal installments in respect of Private Institutes.

The Main feature of the revised Scheme is (i) payment of central assistance to PETCs on contractual basis on per student basis as per the rates provided for in the scheme. (ii) Universities and private institutes to funded on 100% of contractual basis while States owned PETCs will be funded 50% of contractual amount. (iii) The system of deducting committed laibility of the State Government has been done away with. (iv) The income ceiling of candidates eligible for admissions has been raised from Rs. 24,000 per annum to Rs. 44,500 per annum. (v) While the Central Government will give financial assistance for coaching in respect of exams of all-India recruitment character, the. State Governments Civil Services Exams and other subordinate examinations limited to State Government jobs will- not be covered under the scheme.

The expenditure/releases out of the Central share and number of SC/ST students benefited under the Scheme is as follows:-

(Rs. In Crores)

Year	*Allocation*	*Releases*	*No. of Beneficiaries*
1994-95	2.00	2.00	9449
1995-96	3.00	2.05	10323
1996-97	3.00	1.89	N.A.
1997-98	3.00	1.50	N.A.

During the year 1998-99 against the allocation of Rs. 3.00 crores an amount of Rs. 0.92 crores has been released upto Dec., 1998 to State/U.T's.

Centrally sponsored scheme of upgradation of merit for SCs/STs

The objective of the Scheme is to upgrade the merit of Scheduled Castes/Scheduled Tribes students by providing them with facilities for alround development through education in residential schools.

The Scheme of Upgradation of Merit of SC/ST students provides for 100% Central Assistance to States/UTs for arranging remedial and special coaching for Scheduled Castes and Scheduled Tribes students studying in class IX to XII. While remedial coaching aims at removing deficiencies in school subjects, special coaching is provided with a view to prepare students for competitive examinations for entry into professional courses like Engineering and Medical. Scheme of Upgradation of Merit of SC/ST students was started in 1987-88 in the Ministry of Human Resource Development (Department of Education). The scheme was transferred to Ministry of Welfare in the middle of 1993-94. Under this scheme coaching is provided in linguistic skills Science and Mathematics.

The expenditure/ releases out of the Central share and number of SC/ST student benefited under the Scheme is as follows—

(Rs. In Crores)

Year	*Allocation*	*Releases*	*Physical Target (No. of students per class)*	*Achievement (Students Benefited)*
1994-95	1.00	1.00	1000	2336
1995-96	1.00	0.22	1000	884
1996-97	1.00	0.16	1000	280
1997-98	1.00	0.76	1000	609

During the year 1998-99 against the allocation of Rs. 1.00 crores an amount of Rs. 0.85 crore has been released upto Dec., 1998 to States/U.Ts

The Scheme has been modified w.e.f. 1998-99 and the main features of the revised Scheme is—

(i) State/U.T. may use their own discretion in -deciding number and location of schools to be covered under the Scheme.

(ii) Number of awards in respect of each State/U.T. fixed as given under the Scheme, but each State/ U.T. will have a minimum of 5 awards.

(iii) Package grant of Rs. 15,000/- per year per student will be given.

(iv) Besides (iii) above, student with disabilities will be eligible for additional grants as provided for in the Scheme.

Note on the scheme of AID to voluntary organisations for the welfare of scheduled castes

The main purpose behind the Scheme of Aid to Voluntary Organisations for the Welfare of Scheduled Castes is to improve their educational and socio-economic conditions through voluntary efforts.

Assistance is provided for establishing centres and developing services which could equip the SCs with skills to enable them to start income generating activities on their own or get gainfully employed. Grants in aid to voluntary organisations under the Scheme is given mainly for the following purposes:

(a) Opening of schools and hostels, ashram schools, training in Arts and Crafts and any other income generating skills.

(b) Running Balwaries and Bal Kendras i.e. creches to look after the deprived children of Scheduled Caste Communities.

(c) For providing medical facilities to Scheduled Castes through establishement of Hospitals or Mobile Dispensaries.

The Scheme has been modified and renamed as Grant in aid to Voluntary organisations working for Scheduled Castes. The main objective has been to simplify the procedure and also to expand the scope of the scheme.

In the revised scheme, focus has been given for

(i) Scheduled Castes persons with disability to receive special attention,

(ii) Scheduled Castes beneficiaries living in North-Eastern Region to be given focussed attention;

(iii) Programmes for Scheduled Castes Women to receive priority.

The revised scheme has been circulated to all the concerned.

Details of allocation vis a vis expenditure during last three years and till date:—

(Rs. in Lakhs)

Year	*Budget Allocation*	*Expenditure*
1995-96	2033	1084
1996-97	1733	1000
1997-98	2000	1003
1998-99	1800	1420
		(As on 31.12.98)

The section is working with the foHowing staff:

i. Section Officer 1

ii. Assistants 3

iii.	UDC	1
iv.	LDC	2 (one post is vacant)

There are about 425 on going organisations who are running about 650 projects for SCs. The section is dealing with the cases of grant in aid for all these projects. In addition, 505 fresh proposals are, pending in the section which are awaiting consideration. These proposals could not be considered as the funds allocated for fresh proposals have exhausted. The work load in the section has tremendously increased and it is very difficult to cope up with the work of the Section. The Voluntry organisations getting grant in aid under the scheme of Aid to- Voluntary, organisation during 1998-99.

Centrally sponsored scheme of implementation of protection of Civil Rights Act, 1955 and the scheduled castes and the scheduled tribes (Prevention of Atrocities) Act, 1989

The Protection of Civil Rights Act, 1955 was enacted in furtherance of Article 17 of the Constitution by which untouchability was abolished and its practice in any from forbidden. Further in order to check and deter crimes against SCs AND STs by persons belonging to other communities, the Scheduled Castes and the Scheduled Tribes (Prevention of Atrocties) Act 1989 was brought into force from January, 1990. These enactments have extended the concept of positive discrimination in favour of SCs and STs to the field of criminal Law in as much as they generally prescribe penalties that are more stringent than for corresponding offences under the Indian Penal Code (IPC) And other laws. Comprehensive Rules were also notified under the POA Act in 1995 which lay down, in particular, enhanced scales for relief and rehabilitation. These statutes require the State Governments/UT Administrations to undertake various measures for preventing and penalising untouchability practices and atrocities and generally, for effective implementation of the Acts. The Central Government is required to coordinate measures taken by the State and UTs.

Under Centrally Sponsored Scheme, financial assistance is provided to the State Governments in the ratio of 50:50 (100% to UTs) over and above the committed liability to be borne by them for all measures they have undertaken or propose to undertake for the effective implementation of these Acts and the Rules. Such measures may include strengthening of the administrative, enforcement and judicial machinery, publicity, and relief and rehabilitation. The year-wise position of sanction of Central Assistance is as follows:

(Rs. in crores)

Year	*Central Assistance*
1994-95	9.75
1995-96	15.37
1996-97	12.50
1997-98	16.47
1998-99	14.28 (As on 30.11.998)

During 1998-99 a sum of Rs. 15.50 crores have been allocated for the scheme, This Ministry also made special efforts during the year to release adhoc central assistance to the State Governments for timely disbursment of relief to the victims of atrocities.

Implementation of protection of Civil Rights Act, 1955

Section 15-A of the PCR Act requires the State Govts. to take measures to ensure that the rights arising from the abolition of untouchability are made available to, and are availed of, by persons subjected to any disability arising out of untouchability. These measures may include:

(i) the provision of adequate facilities, including legal aid, to the persons subjected to any disability arising out of "untouchability" to enable them to avail themselves of such rights;

(ii) the appointment of officers for initiating or exercising supervision over prosecution for the contravention of the provisions of this Act;

(iii) the setting up of Special Courts for the trial of offences under this Act.

(iv) The setting up of Committees at such appropriate levels as the State Governments may think fit to assist the State Government in formulating or implementing such measures;

(v) Provision for a periodic survey of the working of the provisions of this Act with a view to suggesting measures for the better implementation of the provisions of this Act.

(vi) The identification of the areas where persons are under any disability arising out of "untouchability" and adoption of such measures as would ensure the removal of such disability from such areas.

In most States/UTs, Committees/Special Cells/ Squads and/or officers -have been constituted or appointed at different levels for supervising various aspects of the implementation of the Act. Most States/UTs also have legal aid schemes under which assistance is provided to SC/ST persons in various kind of cases indirectly related to untouchability offences and atrocities, such as land disputes, etc. although some States provide free legal aid irrespective of income, some others prescribed income ceilings for eligibility.

The establishment or even specification of Special Courts is not mandatory under the PCR Act, though the Act does stipulate that most categories of offences would be triable by Judicial Magistrates (First Class) or Metropolitan Magistrates. Some States have designated existing Courts as Special Courts. Exclusive Special

Courts have also been set up to try offences under the Act in the States of Andhra Pradesh (22), Bihar (4), Karnataka (4), Madhya Pradesh (4) and Rajasthan (6).

Though the prevalance of untouchability is on the decline, yet its prevalance is still reported, in one form or "he other, in some parts of the country viz. Andhra Pradesh, Bihar, Goa, Gujarat, Haryana, Himachal Pradesh, Jammu & Kashmir, Karnataka, Kepla, Madhya Pradesh, Maharashtra, Orissa, Punjab, Rajasthan, Tamil Nadu, Uttar Pradesh, Delhi and Pondicherry. Over the years, the registration of cases under the Protection of Civil Rights Act, 1955 has been declining as will be seen from the follwoing:-

Year	*No. of cases registered under PCR Act*
1994	1794
1995	1599
1996	1489
1997	1304
1998	537 (provisional)

Working of the scheduled castes and the scheduled tribes (Prevention of Atrocities) Act, 1989

In order to check and deter crimes against SCs/STs by persons belonging to other communities, the SCs and STs Prevention of Atrocities (POA) Act, 1989 was brought into force from 30.1.90.

The POA act defines certain categories of offences against SCs and the STs as 'atrocities' for the purposes of the Act, Comprehensive Rules were also notified under the POA Act in 1995 which lay down, among other things, norms for relief and rehabilitation.

The POA Act prescribes punishments which are higher than for corresponding offences under the Indian Penal Code.

Under the POA Act, State Governments are required to undertake various measures which may include:

(i) provision of adequate facilities, including legal aid;

(ii) travelling and maintenance expenses to victims and witnesses;

(iii) appointment of officers for initiating and exercising supervision over prosecutions;

(iv) setting up of Committees at different levels for formulation or implementation of such measures;

(v) periodic surveys of the working of the Act with a view to suggesting measures for better implementation,

(vi) identification of atrocity-prone areas, 'and adoption of measures to ensure the safety of SCs/ STs in such areas.

(vii) relief and rehabilftation to victims/dependents of atrocities.

Provisions rega.dingg special courts

For the purpose of speedy trial, Section .14 of the POA Act requires the State Governments to specify, with the concurrence of the Chief Justice of the respective High Courts, a Court of Sessions for each district as a Special Court to try offences under the Act.

All States/UTs (except for the predominantly tribal States of Arunachal Pradesh and Nagaland) have specified existing Sessions Courts for each district as Special Courts.

. addition, although this is not mandatory under the Act, Six States namely, Andhra Pradesh (3), Gujarat(3), Karnataka(4), Madhya Pradesh(25), Rajasthan(16) and Tamil Nadu(4) have also set up separate Special Courts exclusively for trying cases under the SCs & STs (Prevention of Atrocities) Act, 1989.

Number of atrocity cases

The data on atrocity cases against the SCs and STs in the country during 1997 as maintained by National Crimes Record Bureau of Ministry of Home Affairs.

Monitoring of point 11(A) of twenty point programme

Performance of Point 11(A) of Twenty Point Programme related to "Justice of Scheduled Castes" is monitored, inter-alia, in terms of the number of Scheduled Castes families assisted through various income generation schemes.

During VIII Plan 118.67 lakh Scheduled Caste families were assisted against a target of 127.6 lakhs Scheduled Caste families showing 93% achievements. During IX Plan 124 lakh Scheduled Caste families have been targetted to be assisted.

During 1997-98, 20.66 lakh Scheduled Caste families have been assisted against a target of 25.95 families.The year-wise targets and achievements during the Eight and Ninth Plan period are as given below:—

	Sc Families assisted		
Period	*Target*	*Achievement*	*%*
1992-93	25,95,568	20,65,987	79.60
1993-94	25,24,800	23,23,722	92.60
1994-95	25,83,500	26,96,412	104.37
1995-96	25,62,000	24,82,075	96.88
1996-97	25,00,100	22,98,,900	91.95
IX Plan	124,00,000		
1997-98	25,95,568	20,65,987	79.60
1998-99	24,35,030	11,61,000	

Research and training scheme

Ministry of Social Justice and Empowerment invities

research proposals from Government and non Govermental organisations and various research Institutes/Universities for conducting evaluation studies regarding various developmental programmes for Schelduled Castes. Details of research studies, seminars/ workshops sponsored under the scheme during 1997-98 and current financial year are as follow:-

Year	*Research Studies*	*Seminars Workshops*
1997-98	40	29
1998-99	22	Nil
(Upto Nov., 98)		

The studies undertaken during VIII Plan under the scheme cover wide range of aspects of development of Scheduled castes including the performance of Scheduled Castes Finance and Development Corporations functioning in various States, implementation of Post-matric Scholarship, Prematric Scholarship for the children of those engaged in unclean occupations, hostels for Scheduled Caste boys and girls and Coaching and Allied Scheme.

Year-wise out-lay and expenditure under the scheme during 1997-98 and during current year is as shown below— *(Rs in lakhs)*

Year	*Outlay*	*Expenditure*
1997-98	50.00	33.00
1998-99	190.00	19.00
		(Upto Nov., 98)

Effectiveness of Special Component Plans in States and its impact on the development of Scheduled Castes, liberation of scavengers scheme and, its effcctveness in achieving occupational mobility trend among Scheduled Caste people, aspirations of Scheduled Castes and various other subjects have also been taken up under the scheme.

The Research Studies are sponsored with an aim to improve the formulation and implementation of educational and economic development plans etc. for development of Scheduled Castes.

The scheme is implemented under the guidance of a Research Advisory Committee of the Ministry.

Dr. Ambedkar foundation

Dr. Ambedkar Foundation was established by the Government of India under the aegis of the Ministry of Welfare on March 24, 1992 as a registered society under the Societies Registration Act, 1860.

The Foundation has been entrusted with the responsibility to manage, administer and carry on the important and long term Schemes and Programmes identified during the Centenary Celebrations of Bharat Ratna Baba Saheb Dr. B. R. Ambedkar.

The important Schemes and Programmes of the Foundation are:

(i) Dr. Ambedkar National Public Library in Delhi.

(ii) Dr. Ambedkar Chairs in Universities/ Institutions for research on the thoughts and ideals of Baba Saheb.

(iii) Dr. Ambedkar National Award for Social Understanding and Upliftment of Weaker Sections.

(iv) Dr. Ambedkar International Award for Social Change, Harmony, Equity, Justice and Human Dignity for- the exploited and the under-privileged.

(v) Publication of the Collected Works of Baba Saheb

Dr. Ambedkar in Hindi and other Indian languages.

(vi) Putting up Memorial for Dr. Ambedkar at 26, Alipur Road, Delhi.

(vii) Various General Activities like organising seminars. Conferences, Workshops, Exhibitions and Melas on Dr. Ambedkar, his life and mission.

The present position of the above Schemes and Programmes is as follows:

Dr. Ambedkar national public library

Land for the Library has been allotted by the Ministry of Urban Affairs & Employment in the Institutional Areas between Raisina Road and Dr. Rajendra Prasad Road. Out of the five Bungalows in the allotted area, actual possession of one Bungalow has already been taken over and possession of the rest of the Bunglows are expected to be obtained shortly. Since the working Group which was constituted in 1994 could not prepare a proper design and plan for the Library, it has since been decided to appoint an Architect Designer for the purpose. An amount of Rs. 5.50 crores has already been provided to the Foundation for this project. The project is likely to cost about Rs. 100 crores. As per the existing scheme and annual grant of Rs. 200 lakhs is being released to the Chairs for meeting their yearly expenditure. In addition, in the beginning a one-time grant of Rs. 50,000/- is also provided for meeting the initial equipment/ establishment expenditure. A proposal is under consideration to increase the amount of grant to be provided to the Chairs as well as to set up more Chairs.

Dr. Ambedkar overseas fellowship

Four Dr. Ambedkar Overseas Fellowships are being awarded every year for students since the year 1992-93, to pursue their studies abroad in the field of Law Economics, Sociology and International Relations. The

Scholarships are awarded solely on the basis of merit and so far 12 scholars have been provided fellowships for the year 1992-93, 1993-94 and 1994-95. The Governing Body of the Foundation in their meeting held on 14.9.97 has reviewed this Scheme and decided to discontinue it. However, the Scholars who have already been sent abroad and are making good progress will be allowed to continue their course.

Dr. Ambedkar natinal award for social understanding and upliftment of weaker sections

Dr. Ambedkar National Award for the year 1993 has been presented to NISWASS of Orissa and the Award for the year 1994 has been given away to Rayat Shikshan Sansthan of Satara, Maharashtra. Nominations received for the Award for the years 1995 and 1996 have been processed and are being put up for selection before the National Jury which has been reconstituted recently.

Dr. Ambedkar International award for social change

Dr. Ambedkar International Award for Social change has also been instituted. The award which carries a cash prize of Rs. 1.50 million and a citation, will be conferred every year on eminent Individual(s) Group(s)/Organisation(s)/ Institution(s) who have contributed in the light against inequality and injustice to bring about social changes. The jury for the Award has been constituted, and necessary actions are underway for calling nominations.

Collected works of Baba Saheb Dr. Ambedkar in hindi and other Indian languages

The writings and speeches of Dr. Ambedkar published in English by the Govt. of Maharashtra have been taken up by the Foundation for Translation and Publication in Hindi, Bengali, Gujarati, Kannada, Malayalam, Oriya, Punjabi, Tamil, Telugu, Marathi, Asameese and Urdu. Eleven Volumes in Hindi, eight in Tamil, four in Punjabi, ten in Bengali, fifteen in Gujarati, five in Kannada, eight in Telugu, four in Malayalam and two in Oriya have been brought out the work in other languages is in progress. Small low priced booklets containing Dr. Ambedkar's Philosophy and thoughts are being brought out. An amount of Rs. 6.44 crores has been provided to the Foundation for this project.

Memorial for Dr. Ambedkar

The Govt. had resolved to construct a Memorial for Dr. Ambedkar at 26, Alipur Road, Delhi where he had lived and attained Parinirvan, Pursuant to this, an amount of Rs. 10.00 crores was released to the Foundation during 1996-97 out of which Rs. 7.12 crores as 80% of the estimated cost of acquisition of Rs. 8.90 crores has been released to the Govt. of NCT Delhi as per their request. The Delhi Govt. have already issued Notifications under section (4) and subsequently under section 6 of the Land Acquisition Act, The actual possession of the land expected to be obtained shortly and the construction of the Memorial will be commenced immediately thereafter. Already a high-level Committee has been constituted to conceptualise the Memorial as well as to firm up its cost estimates.

Other activities of the foundation

In addition to these Schemes aims and objectives of Dr. Ambedkar Foundation also include other activities such as holding of National/Regional Seminars/ Conferences/ Workshops, lectures and Symposia on socio-economic issues, holding of Annual Functions on 14th April and 6th December to commemorate Birth Anniversary and Mahaparinivaran Diwas of Baba Saheb and publication pamphlets/periodicals. The Foundation is bringing out a quarterly, viz Dr. Ambedkar Foundation Patrika and the first issue has already been released. The work on the subsequent issues is in progress. It is observed that at present there is a lot of vitification/mis-information campaign going on against Baba Saheb. To counter this and to bring out facts in the correct perspective, a Research Cell has been constituted in the Foundation which has already begun its work.

Feature film on Baba Saheb

A full length Film on Dr. Ambedkar is being produced by the National Film Development Corporation. The shooting has already been completed and the post shooting work has since begun. The film is expected to be released shortly.

5

Tribal Development

India has people of diverse races and cultures living within it. The tribal communities belonging to various races are spread across the country, mainly in the forest and hilly regions. The word Tribe means a group of families bound together by kinship, usually descendening from mythical or legendary ancestor, living in a common region, speaking a common dialect and having common historical past. The essential characteristics of these communities are primitive traits, geographical isolation, distinctive culture, shyness of contact with out siders and economic backwardness. According to Article 342 of the Constitution of India the Scheduled Tribes are the tribes or tribal communities or part of or group within tribes and tribal communities which have been declared as such by the President by the public notification. More than 70 percent of the Scheduled Tribes population is concentrated in seven States of Madhya Pradesh, Maharashtra, Orissa, Bihar, Andhra Pradesh, West Bengal and Gujarat. No community has been specified as Scheduled Tribe in respect of States of Haryana & Punjab & UTs of Chandigarh, Delhi & Pondicherry.

Profile of scheduled tribes

According to 1991 Census the total population of the country was 846 million, out of which the population of Scheduled Tribe was 68 millions, constituting 8.08

percent of the country's total population 42.02% of the ST population were main workers of them, 54-50% were cultivators and 32.69% were agricultural labourers. Thus about 87% of the main workers, were engaged in primary sector activities. As against the national average of 52%, the literacy rate of Scheduled Tribes is around 29.60%. More than three quarters of Sch. Tribe women are illiterate. These disparities are compounded by higher drop-out rates in formal in their representation in higher education being disproportionately low. Not surprisingly, the cumulative effect has been , that the proportion of Scheduled Tribes below the poverty line is substantially higher than the national average. The estimate of poverty made by Planning Commission education resulting for the year 1993-94 shows that 51.92% rural and 41.14% urban ST population was still living below the poverty line.

Constitutional provisions

The Constitution of India has laid responsibility on the shoulders of both the State Govt. as well as Central Govt. so far as development of STs is concerned. Article 46 states that the State shall promote with special care the educational and economic interests of the people and in particular of the Scheduled Castes and Scheduled Tribes and shall protect them from social injustice and all other forms of exploitation.

Article 16(4) and 16(4A) empower the State to make provision for reservation in the appointment for posts in favour of Scheduled Tribes along with other categories both in direct recruitments and in promotions. Article 164(l) provides that in the States of Bihar, Madhya Pradesh and Orissa there shall be a Minister incharge of Tribal Affairs who may in addition be in charge of welfare of Scheduled Castes and Backward Classes or any other work.

Article 244(1) provides that the provisions of Fifth Schedule shall apply to the Administration and control of Scheduled areas and Schedule Tribes. Article 275(1) provides that Grant in aid would be provided out of Consolidated fund of India to the States to meet the cost of such schemes of development as may be undertaken by them with the approval of Government of India for the purpose of promoting the welfare of schedule Tribes or raising the level of Schedule Areas.

Articles 330 and 332 provide reservation for Schedule Tribes and Schedule Castes in Lok Sabha and State Legislative Assemblies respectively. Under Article 338 a National Commission for Scheduled Castes and Scheduled Tribes has been constituted which acts as a watch dog for safeguarding the interests of Scheduled Castes and Scheduled Tribes.

The Fifth Schedule to the Constitution empowers the Governor's of States having Schedule Areas therein to make regulations for good government and to modify the State and Central legislations regarding their applicability, Paragraph 4 of the Fifth Schedule provides for setting up of a Tribes advisory. Council which shall advise on such matters pertaining to welfare and advancement of Schedule Tribes which are referred to it by the Governor. Sixth Schedule to the Constitution which is applicable to the States of Assam, Meghalaya, Mizoram and Tripura, provides a mechanism of administering the local issues by the tribals themselves.

Initiatives undertaken by T.D. division during the year 1998

All the Central/Centrally Sponsored Schemes which are under implementation will continue during Ninth Plan. Revision of the schemes have been made after consultation with the Planning Commission and the Ministry of Finance. The Schemes are being implemented according to revised norms.

(i) A new central sector scheme for the development of Primitive Tribal Groups has been introduced during current financial year. Under this scheme cent percent assistance would be available to Integrated Tribal Development Projects (ITDPs), Tribal Research Institute (TRI) and Non-Governmental Organisations (NGOs) for undertaking activities such as awareness generation and confidence building, training for skill development of tribal youth organisations of self help groups and provision of services/inputs not covered by any existing scheme.

(ii) Scheduled Areas and Scheduled Tribes Commission It has been decided to set up 11 member Scheduled Areas and Scheduled Tribes Commission under Article 339(1) of the Constitution, The main objective of the Commission is to examine the existing TSP strategy and to suggest alternative arrangements, if necessary.

(iii) National Institute for Training and Research In Tribal Affairs It has been decided to set up a National Institute for Training and Research in Tribal Affairs at Delhi. The main purpose of setting up a National Institute is to coordinate research activities of 14 TRIs in various states and to assist the Ministry of Social Justice and Empowerment in formulating policies and programmes relating to protective laws, self-determination, socio-political movements, health, literacy, shifting cultivation, scheduling and descheduling, displacement and rehabilitation. There is also a need for training of different categories of public and service personnel in Tribal Development matters, which will also be coordinated by this Institute.

(iv) Revision of the Schemes have been initiated after consultation with the Planning Commission and the Ministry of Finance.

(v) Revision of Norms of the Scheme of Grant-in-Aid to Voluntary Organisation working for the Welfare of the Scheduled Tribes have been made raising the cost heads to a realistic and workable level.

Tribal Sub-Plan (TSP Strategy)

In order to accelerate socio-economic development of the Scheduled Tribes and their protection against the exploitation, Government of India has adopted a seperate straegy known at the TSP, since the Fifth Five Year Plan with the objective of (i) bringing them on par with other section of the Society and (ii) to protect them from exploitation by various vested interest groups. TSP strategy is in operation in 13 States, namely Andhra Pradesh, Assam, Bihar, Gujrat, Himachal Pradesh, Jammu & Kashmir, Karnataka, Kerala, Madhya Pradesh, Maharashtra, Manipur, Orissa, Rajasthan, Sikkim, Tamil Nadu, Tripura, Uttar Pradesh and West Bengal and two Union Territories, namely Andaman and Nicobar Islands and Daman & Diu. In order to fulfil the above objective, 194 Integrated Tribal Development Projects (ITDPs) have been set up in blocks or groups of blocks where the ST population is more than 50% of the total population. Modified Area Development Approach (MADA) Pockets have been formed in groups of villages having population of 10,000 or more with, 50% or more tribal population, 252 MADA Pockets have been created. In addition, 79 Clusters have also been formed for groups of villages having population of 5,000 or more where STs constitute more than 50% of the population. 75 Primitive Tribal Groups (PTGs) have been identified in 15 States/ UTs on the basis of pre-agricultural level of technology and extremely low levels of literacy.

Special central assistance (SCA) for tribal sub-plan

The Special Central Assistance is given by the Ministry of Welfare to !he Tribal Sub-Plan State Governments/UT Administrator to fill in the gaps in, their financial outlays. The SCA is to be utilised in conjunction with the TSP flow with a view to meet the gaps which are not otherwise taken care of by the State Plan. It is basically meant for family-oriented income generating schemes in sectors of agriculture, horticulture, minor irrigation, soil-conservation, animal husbandry, forest, education, cooperatives, fisheries, villages and small industries and Minimum Needs Programme. The criteria for allocation of Special Central Assistance have been fixed on the basis of certain norms for ITDP, MADA Pockets, Clusters, Primitive Tribal Groups and Dispersed Tribal Groups. The allocation and expenditure for the years 1992-93 to 1997-98 is as follows.

(Rs. in Lakhs)

Year	*Allocation*	*Amount Released*
1	2	3
8th Plan (1992-97)	1,25,000	1,47,985
1992-93	25,000	25,000
1993-94	29,500	29,485
1994-95	27,500	27,500
1995-96	33,000	33,000
9th Plan		
(1997-2002)		
1996-97	33,000	33,000
1997-98	33,000	33,961,
1998-99	38,000	29,308 (as on 15.2.1999)

Tribal sub plan of central ministries

The Tribal sub Plan strategy seeks to ensure adequate flow of funds not only from the State Plan funds, institutional finances and central sector/centrally sponsored schemes of the Ministry of Social Justice & Empowerment, but also. from all the Central Ministries/ Departments.

The Planning Commission and the Ministry of Social Justice & Empowerment send letters to all the concerned Central Ministries/Departments every year on the need for quantification of funds from their annual plan in accordance with the population percentage of the Scheduled Tribes in the country.

The details of quantification of funds made by various Central Ministries during the year 199899 is given below—

(Rs. in Crores)

S. No.	Ministry/Deptt.	Total outlay	Flow to TSP	%age
1.	M/o. Commerce	203.80	20.92	10.26
2.	D/o. Food & Civil Supplies	0.32	0.03	9.38
3.	D/o. Biotechnology	–	0.50	–
4.	Rural Electrification Corporation Ltd.	–	48.00	–
5.	M/o. Power (Kutir Jyoti Scheme)	–	40.00	–
6.	D/o. Agriculture	1941.00	97.53	–
7.	M/o Labour	6.08	2.58	42.11
8.	D/o. Youth Affairs & Sports	NA	2.56	–

Grants under first proviso to article 275(1) of the constitution

The Ministry of Social Justice and Empowerment gives grants to 18 Tribal Sub-Plan (TSP) and 4 Tribal majority States under First Proviso to Article 275(l) of the constitution to meet the cost of such projects for Tribal Development as may be undertaken by the State Government for raising the level of administration of the Scheduled Areas therein to that of the rest of the State.

The funds allocated and amount released since VIII Five Year Plan are as follows.,

(Rs. In Lakhs)

Year	*Allocation*	*Amount released*
8th Plan (1992-97)	20,000.00	20,000.00
1992-93	4,000.00	4,000.00
1993-94	7,500.00	7,500.00
1994-95	7,500.00	7,500.00
1995-96	7,500.00	7,500.00
1996-97	7,500.00	7,500.00
9th Plan (1997-2002)		
1997-98	7,500.00	7,500.00
1998-99	7,500.00	5,385.22

In the case of the funds provided to the States/Union Territories under SCA and first provision to Article 275(l) the Ministry has devised a mechanism of monitoring under which quarterly reports are obtained from the States/UTs on utilisation of funds for various activities and the physical achievements in terms of beneficiaries assisted for their socioeconomic development.

Residential Schools: Since 1997-98, it has been decided to utilise a part of the funds under Article 275(l) of the Constitution for setting up 100 Residential Schools from Class 6 to 12 in States and U.Ts. for tribal students.

For this purpose, it has been decided to provide Rs. 250.00 crores during the 9th Five Year Plan out of the funds available under Article 275(1) of the Constitution. The objective of setting up of the Residential Schools is to provide quality education to the Tribal Students. This will enable the tribal children to avail of the facility of reservation in higher and professional education courses as well as in higher levels of jobs in the government and Public Sector undertakings. The State Government have been requested to set up a Society on the pattern of Andhra Pradesh Tribal Welfare Residential and Ashram Educational Institutions Society (Regd.) Hyderabad. Each of the 100 schools would be provided non-recurring grant of Rs. 2.5 Crores. Out of the total allocation of Rs. 75.00 Crores during 1997-98, Rs. 50.00 Crores has been released to 22 States for opening 50 Schools, and it is proposed to release Rs. 25.00 Crores during 1998-99 to the States where the Societies have been registered and proposal for setting up of the Residential schools have been formulated.

Governors report

To provide an objective evaluation of the developments in scheduled areas, the Governor of each State having scheduled area therein, is required to make a report to the President regarding administration of scheduled areas in that State. The scheduled areas have been declared in eight states namely Andhra Pradesh, Bihar, Gujarat, Himachal Pradesh, Maharashtra, Madhya Pradesh, Orissa and Rajasthan.

The Governor's report has to give an unbiased assessment of the situation in scheduled areas highlighting, interalia, various measures taken for upgradation of administration of such areas, implementation of the protective laws, matters referred to the Tribes Advisory Council (TAC) and their recommendation etc. It has been generally observed that the Governor's report are normally a summary of achievements of State Governments in tribal development. Little efforts is made to qualitatively evaluate and critically analyse the problems of scheduled areas in these reports.

The states are required to send the Governor's report within six months of the closing of the financial year i.e. by the 30th September of each year. However, these reports are generally not received in time. The following table gives the position of reports which have not been received in the Ministry.

Position of governor's report upto January 1999

Sl.	*Name of States*	*Year for which the Report No. have not been received*
1.	Andhra Pradesh	1996-97 & 1997-98
2.	Bihar	1992-93 to 1997-98
3.	Gujarat	1997-98
4.	Madhya Pradesh	1997-98
5.	Maharashtra	1996-97 & 1997-98
6.	Orissa	1996-97 & 1997-98
7.	Rajasthan	1997-98
8.	Himachal Pradesh	1997-98

Tribes advisory council (TAC)

An important mechanism for tribal development and welfare, is the Tribes Advisory Council under Para 4 of the fifth Schedule of the Constitution. Eight States having Scheduled areas namely Andhra Pradesh, Bihar, Gujarat, Himachal Pradesh, Maharashtra, Madhya Pradesh, Orissa and Rajasthan and two non Scheduled Area States, namely Tamil Nadu and West Bengal, have constituted Tribes Advisory Councils.

The TACs consist of not more than twenty members of whom as many as three-fourths shall be the representatives of Scheduled Tribes in the Legislative assembly of the States.

As per the guidelines issued by the Ministry of Social Justice & Empowerment, the Tribes Advisory Council should meet atleast twice a year with adequate preparation to make them effective. It is only then that the TACs can become a meaningful and important forum representing tribal interest.

Research and training

Under the Schemes of Research and Training, the Ministry provides financial assistance for three components, (i) Grants to Tribal Research Institutes (TRIs) of the State Governments on sharing basis of fifty-fifty of plan schemes, (ii) Award Of Research Fellowship in various aspects of Tribal Development (Doctoral/Post Doctoral Fellowship) to the students who are registered in Universities on 100% basis and (iii) Research Projects of All-India or Inter-State nature. The grant is provided on 100% basis to Governmental and Non-Governmental Institutes/ Organisation for conducting research and evaluation studies.

Grant to tribal research institutes

Tribal Research Institutes have been set up by State Governments to conduct Research and Evaluation, Seminars and Workshops on various subjects relevant to tribals, to provide training and orientation to State Government officials and to give support to State Governments for preparation of Tribal Sub Plan. Some institutes are also having Museums attached to them for exhibiting Tribal artifacts. Under the Scheme central grants are given on 50:50 basis to the Tribal Research Institutes.

At present 14 Tribal Research Institutes in the states of Andhra Pradesh, Assam, Bihar, Gujarat, Kerala, Maharashtra, Madhya Pradesh, Orissa and Rajasthan, Tamil Nadu, Uttar Pradesh, West Bengal, Manipur and Tripura have been set up. This Ministry has also considered to establish a National Institute for Research and Training in Tribal Affairs at New Delhi. For 1998-99 a sum of Rs. 650.00 Lakhs have been allocated out of which Rs. 109.16 Lakhs have been released upto 17th February 1999.

Award of research fellowship in various aspects of tribal development (Doctoral/Post Doctoral Fellowship)

The Ministry of Social Justice & Empowerment is giving grants for Research Fellowship on 100% basis to students/scholars, who are registered with a University for working on Tribal Development programmes/ problems. The rates of Fellowship for doctoral and Post doctoral courses were Rs. 1800 per month and Rs. 2200 per month respectively, which stands revised to Rs. 2800 and Rs. 3200 respectively. In Addition an annual contingency grant of Rs. 7000 is allowed.

Research projects of all-India or inter-state nature (Scheduled Tribes)

The scheme relating to grant for Research and Evaluation project is being operated by the Ministry. Grants upto Rs. 1.50 lakhs per Project for a period of 8 months were given to Non-Government Organisation, which has been revised to Rs. 2.50 Lakhs per project for a period of 8 to 12 months (w.e.f. I st Dec. 1998)., During 1997-98 a -sum of Rs. 50.00 Lakhs has been budgeted but due to instruction of Finance Ministry, the Budget was revised to Rs. 15.00 Lakhs, the whole amount was released for new research proposals. During 1998-99 a sum of Rs. 50.00 Lakhs has been allocated out of which Rs. 25.00 Lakhs has been released upto 17th Feb. 1999.

Girls hostels for scheduled tribes

The scheme of girls hostel, which was started in the Third Plan, is a useful instrument for spreading education among ST girls, whose literacy still stands at 18.19% as per 1991 census against the general female literacy of 39.23%. Under the scheme, Central Assistance is given to the States/UTs for construction of now hostel buildings and/or extention of existing hostels. This is a Centrally sponsored Scheme where the cost of construction of the hostel building is equally shared between the Centre and the State in the ratio of 50:50. In case of UTs, the Central Government bears the entire cost of the building. The cost of construction is based on the State PWD schedule of rate or local CPWD schedule of rates, which ever is lower. Maintenance of the hostel is the responsibility of the concerned States/UTs. The number of seats in a hostel is limited generally to 100. The hostels are -for ST girls in middle and high schools, colleges and universities.

Out of Rs. 1405 lakhs provided in the Annual Budgets from 1994-95 to 1997-98, Rs. 1370.28 Lakhs was released to the States/UTs. for construction of 261 hostels. During the year 1998-99, the Budget provision for the scheme is Rs. 800 lakhs and an amount of Rs. 360.66 lakhs has been released for 46 hostels up to 15.2.99.

Boys hostels for scheduled tribes

This scheme was introduced in 1989-90 for construction of boys hostels. The norms followed are the same as those for the girls hostel.

Out of Rs. 1405 lakhs provided in the annual budgets from 1994-95 to 1997-98, an amount of Rs. 1250.69 lakhs was released to State/UTs For construction of 282 hostels. In the current year 1998-99, budget provision for the scheme is Rs. 800 lakhs and an amount of Rs. 531.44 lakhs has been released for construction of 15 hostels up to 15th February, 1999.

Ashrarn school in tribal sub-plan area

The scheme of Ashram School, a Centrally Sponsored Scheme, was launched in 1990-91 with an objective to extend educational facilities through residential schools for ST students. The funding for the scheme is done on matching (50:50) contribution basis with the States/UTs. Cent percent assistance is however, given to UTs. The scheme covers primary, secondary and senior secondary level of education.

Out of Rs. 1350 lakhs provided in the Annual Budgets during 1994-95 to 1998-99, an amount of Rs. 1386.98 lakhs was released to the State/UTs for construction of 297 schools. During the current year, Budget provision is Rs. 900 lakhs and an amount of Rs. 634.64 lakhs has been released for construction of 27 Ashram schools up to 15th February, 1999.

Vocational training centres in tribal area

The main aim of this scheme is to develop the skills of the tribal youth in order to gain employment/self-employment opportunities. The scheme was introduced in 1992-93 as Central Sector Scheme and is implemented through the State Governments. The capacity of the vocational training centres is 50 with hostel facility for 25 of them. Each centre is to have a provision for training in 3 trades out of identified trades, the course of each trade being for a duration of 4 months, At the end of one years' training the trainee is to be attached to a master craftsman for a period of 3 months to sharpen his skills through practical experience. After this, the trainee is expected to emerge as a multi-skilled person capable of self employment. There is residential schools.

The Budget provision for this scheme from 1994-95 to 1997-98 was Rs. 985 lakhs and an amount of Rs. 687 lakhs was released for setting up of educational complexes. During the current financial year, the Budget provision is Rs. 700 lakhs and amount of Rs. 215.43 lakhs has been released up to 15 February, 1999.

Scheme of village grain banks

As part of Government's efforts to prevent deaths of children in remote and backward tribal areas, due to fall in nutrition standards, a scheme of Village Grain Banks has been launched during 199697. A one time grant towards purchase of grains, at the rate of one quintal per family of tribals in such areas, storage facilities for the grain and purchase of -weights and scales is provided by the Ministry of Social Justice and Empowerment, through TRIFED as the channelising agency. The banks will be managed by the Village Committees elected by the beneficiaries themselves, who as members of the bank can borrow grain from the Grain Banks at times of scarcity.

For 1996-97 Rs. 1.50 crores was released for setting up 234 Grain Banks while Rs. 1.80 crores for 281 Grain Banks was released for 1997-98. Allocation for 1998-99 is Rs. 3.00 crores.

Grant-in-aid to Voluntary organisation working for the welfare of scheduled tribes

Various important projects are being implemented by this Ministry through Voluntary Organisations which are working for the Welfare of the Scheduled Tribes. A wide spectrum of projects, which are of direct benefit to the tribals, are considered under this scheme. The projects include Residential Schools, Hostels, Medical Units, Computer Training Units, Shorthand and typing training units, Balwads/Creches (in areas not covered by ICDS Programmes) Libraries and Audio Visual units for dissemination of vital information relevant to the welfare of Scheduled Tribes. The grant is generally restricted to 90% of the approved total cost of project, the balance 10%

is borne by the grantee organisations. There is a budget provision of Rs. 18.00 Crores during 1998-99. A summary of achievements during the last six years is as under:-

(Rs. In Crores)

Year	*Expenditure*	*No. of Vol. Orgn. Assisted*
1992-93	3.55	69
1993-94	4.03	66
1994-95	4.96	79
1995-96	5.30	86
1996-97	5.02	74
1997-98	7.00	113
1998-99	9.92*	161

Grant-in-aid to state tribal development cooperative corporations (TDCCs); and others for minor forest produce (MFP) operations

This is a Central sector Scheme with 100% grant, available to the State Tribal Development Cooperative Corporations; Forest Development Corporations; and Minor Forest Produce (Training & Development) Federation for taking up the minor forest produce operations.

Under this Scheme grants can be utilised by the States for (i) strengthening the share capital base of TDCCs for increasing the volume of procurement of MFPs; (ii) construction of scientific warehouses; (iii) establishing process industries for value addition to MFP items; and (iv) research and Development activities by the Corporations. During the financial year 1997-98 the budget provision of Rs. 8.23 crores was disbursed to 8 State TDCCs. In the current financial year there is a budget provision of Rs. 6.25 crores.

Price support operations to trifed

The price of minor forest produce and surplus agricultural produce are subject to fluctuations. For meeting the unforeseen contingencies of losses because of such fluctuations in the prices and to ensure remunerative prices to the tribal farmers for their produce, the Ministry has been giving financial assistance to the TRIFED to set off part of such losses.

During the last financial year 1997-98, Rs. One crore was released to TRIFED. For the current financial year 1998-99, the budget provision under this scheme is Rs. 4.00 crores.

Investment in the share capital of TRIFED

TRIFED-Tribal Cooperative Marketing Development Federation of India Limited, was setup by the Government of India, under the administrative supervision of the Ministry of Social Justice & Empowerment, in the year 1987, with the prime objective of providing marketing assistance and remunerative prices to Scheduled Tribe Communities for their minor forest produce and surplus agricultural produce and to wean them away from exploitative private traders and middlemen. The Federation is a national level cooperative apex body functioning under the Multi-State Cooperative Societies Act, 1984.

The authorised share capital of TRIFED is Rs. 100.00 Crores and the paid up capital has gone upto Rs. 99.73 crore with the release of Rs. 6.00 crore provided in the budget of 1998-99. Out of Rs. 99.73 crore, the Government of India's contribution is Rs. 99.50 core and the balance Rs. 23.00 lakhs has been contributed by other shareholders.

Point 11 (B) of 20 point programme justice to scheduled tribes

The Scheduled Tribes, numbering 6.7 crores according to

1991 ensus, are the most disadvantaged section of the Indian Society and a large number of them are still below the poverty line. The main thrust of the point 11(b) of -20 point programme, economic assistance is provided to the Sch. Tribe families to enable them to rise above the poverty line. The Sch, Tribe families are assisted through various schemes like Agriculture, Rural Development, Horticulture, Animal Husbandry. Sericulture, Forestry, Small & Cottage Industries, Small business etc., funded from Central, Centrally sponsored and State Government.

The Ministry of Social Justice & Empowerment fixes the targets annually for the 20 TSP States/UTs and also monitors the progress of achievements on monthly basis. For 1998-99, a target of 11.01 lakhs ST families have been fixed for 20 TSP states/UTs. As against this target, till February, 1999. 5.96 lakhs ST families have bean economically assisted.

Central sector scheme for the development of primitive tribal groups (PTGGs)

Based on the pre-agricultural level c technology, low level of literacy and stagnant or diminishing population, 75 tribal communities in 1, States and 1 UT have been identified an categorised as primitive Tribal Groups (PTGs,) For their all round development new central sector scheme for the development i Primitive Tribal Groups has been introduced during current financial year.

Under this scheme cent percent assistant would be available to Integrated Tribal Development projects (ITDPs), Tribal Research Institute (TRI) and Non-Governmental organisations (NGOs) undertaking activities such as awareness generation and confidence building, training for skill development of tribal youth organisation of self help groups and provision of services/inputs not cover by any existing scheme. Central assistance to extent of 100% will be provided to the implement agencies. The Budget allocation for 1998-99 is I 5.00 Crores. An amount of Rs. 2.33 Crores have boon sanctioned upto 15th February 1999.

6

Welfare of Other Backward Classes

Reservation for OBCs

The Supreme Court in its judgement in Indira Sawhney and others vs. Won of India and others (Mandal Case), delivered on 16th November, 1992, upheld the reservation of 27% of vacancies in the civil posts, and services under the Government of India in favour of Other Backward Classes (OBCs) subject to the exclusion of socially advanced persons/sections among them known as "Creamy Layer".

The Supreme Court had directed the Government of India to specify the socio-economic criteria for exclusion of the "Creamy Layer" from the OBCs. The Supreme Court had also directed the Government of India and each of the State Government/UT Administration to set-up a permanent body for recommending upon requests for inclusion and complaints of over-inclusion and under-inclusion in the lists of Other Backward Classes.

Issues arising out of the supreme court judgement

In the above judgement the Supreme Court, besides finally setting the legal position with regard to reservation made the following observations on various aspects of the reservation policy of the Government:—

(i) Reservation of appointments or posts under Article 16(4) is confined to initial appointment only and can not be extended to provide reservation in the matter of promotion;

(ii) The reservation contemplated in Article 16(4) shall not exceed 50%; and

(iii) It is advisable to exclude from the purview of reservation certain services and posts where on account of the nature of duties attached to them or the level at which they obtain, merit alone counts.

Creamy layer

The Supreme Court directed the Central Government as well as the State Governments to specify the basis for applying the relevant and requisite socioeconomic criteria to exclude advanced persons/ sections (Creamy Layer) from OBCs. Accordingly, an amended Government order dated 8th September, 1993 was issued indicating the category of persons/ sections to whom the rule of exclusion will apply.

Creamy layer at a glance

As per the order of the Department of Personnel and Training No. 36012/22-93-Esft. dt. 08-09-1993 the rule of exclusion will apply to son(s) and daughter(s) of persons holding Constitutional positions like President of India, Vice-President of India, Judges of Supreme Court and High Court, Chairman and Members of Union Public service Commission and State Public service Commission, Chief Election Commissioner, Comptroller and Auditor General of India, Parent either of whom is a Class I Officer, Parents other or both of whom is or are in the rank of Colonel and above in the Army and equivalent posts in the Navy and Air Force and the para-military forces.

Families owning irrigated land which, is equal to more than 85% of the ceiling limit in terms of irrigated land as per State land ceiling law.

Persons having gross annual income of Rs. 1.00 lakh or above or possessing wealth, above the exemption limits prescribed in the wealth Tax Act for a period of three consecutive years (income for salaries or agricultural land shall not lie clubbed).

Nottifying the list of other backward classes

The common list of OBCs In respect of 14 States namely Andhra Pradesh, Assam, Bihar, Goa, Gujarat, Haryana, Himachal Pradesh, Karnataka, Kerala, Madhya Pradesh, Maharashtra, Punjab, Tamil Nadu & Uttar Pradesh was published in the Gazette of India extraordinary Part-I, Section 1 No.. 186, dated 13th September, 1993. The second common list of OBCs notified in the Gazette of India extraordinary Part 1, Section 1 No. 163, dated 20th October, 1994 related to States of Orissa, Rajasthan, Tripura & West Bengal. On 25th May, 1995 vide Gazette of India extraordinary Part I Section 1 No. 88, the common list of OBCs in respect of Jammu & Kashmir, Manipur, Sikkim, and NCT of Delhi has also been notified. The Central Government has included/ amended/modified the names of some castes/ communities in the Central List of OBCs in respect of Andhra Pradesh, Kerala, Madhya Pradesh, Maharashtra, Orissa, Tamil Nadu, Tripura, Uttar Pradesh and West Bengal vide Gazette of India, extraordinary Part I section 1 No. 60 dated 11th December, 1996. Besides, the common list of OBCs in respect of LIT of Chandigarh and amendment to OBC list of Uttar Pradesh have been issued on 11-12-1997 and 03-12-1997 respectively.

Releaxed standard

The Government has provided OBC candidates the benefit of relaxed standard in respect of written examination and interview as in the case of SC/ST candidates with effect from 13th October, 1994.

Age relaxation and increased number off attempts for recruitment

On 25th January, 1995 the Government of India has issued instructions relaxing the upper age limit for OBC candidates indirect recruitment by three years and the number of attempts for OBC candidates who are otherwise eligible has been increased to seven in respect of Civil services Examinations.

National commission for backward classes

The National Commission for Backward Classes (NCBC) Act, 1993 was enacted on the direction of the Supreme Court to set up as permanent body for entertaining, examining and recommending upon requests for inclusion and complaints of over-inclusion and under-inclusion in the lists of Other Backward Classes of citizens. As per the provision of the Act, the advice tendered by such body shall ordinarily be binding upon the Government. I Commission was constituted on the 14 August, 1993 for a period of three years. The second National Commission has been constituted on 28th February 1997 for a period of three years.

National backward classes finance & development corporation (NBCFDC)

National Backward Classes Finance & Development Corporation (NBCFDC) was set up by the Government of India under Ministry of Welfare on 13th January, 1992 as a company not for profit under Section 25 of the Company's Act with the objective of providing concessional finance to the members for backward classes living below double the poverty line for their socio-economic development by extending them loans for income generating schemes. The Corporation undertakes:-

(a) to provide additional channel of finance backward

classes for economically a financially viable schemes and projects; and

(b) upgrade the technological and entrepreneur skills of individuals or groups belonging Backward Classes.

The authorised share capital of the Corporation was Rs. 200.00 crores and the same has been now raised to Rs. 700.00 crores. The issued and paid-up capital of the Corporation was Rs. 198.90 on 31.12.98, which has now been raised to Rs. 290.40 crores.

The Corporation has so far sanctioned loans amounting to Rs. 614.31 crores of which Rs. 330.94 crores were disbursed. The number of units covered persons benefitted and the year-wise details of sanctions and disbursements are given below:-

Year	*Amount (Rs. in crores)*		*No. of units*	*No. of beneficiaries*	*Wages Employees*
	Sanctioned	*Disbursed*			
1992-93	33.80	6.90	25821	31939	21302
1993-94	105.07	50.07	71855	76139	47840
1994-95	122.28	68.09	39018	40798	25099
1995-96	29.35	23.35	8084	7794	4300
1996-97	123.33	49.42	61706	72376	30925
1997-98	125.02	70.82	48127	48277	33730
1998-99*	104.13	67.27	20709	28205	15944

Activities which can be financed

NBCFDC can assist a wide range of income generating activities for employment generation to the members of Backward Classes in various sectors as, follows:

(a) Agricultural and Allied activities;

(b) Artisan and Traditional occupations;

(c) Technical Trades-Self- Employment;

(d) Small Scale and tiny Industry;
(e) Small Business; and
(f) Transport services;

These are illustrative and not exhaustive and each scheme may cover a number of identical units.

The Corporation has put great emphasis on training and education as the Corporation in furtherance of its objective spent about Rs. 119.40 lakh as grant-in-aid for 3198 beneficiaries out of which Rs. 30.15 lakh have been provided during 1998-99 upto 31-12-1998.

During the year 1998-99, Corporation continued its concerted efforts in identifying the systems deficiencies and taking corrective measures towards bringing about transparency in its operations.

Frequent field visits are being conducted by the Corporation to assist the SCAs in removing impediments in smooth implementation of Corporation's schemes. Corporation has been sending response cards to the beneficiaries submitted by the SCAs. Further one major scheme in each State is being evaluated through accredited institution, in order to get requisite feed back of the impact of Corporation schemes.

The Corporation has continued its thrust on recovery of loan from SCAs. The Corporation has recovered Rs. 11785.40 lakh as on date. The present repayment percentage is 80 per cent as compared to 74 per cent in 1997-98. Further due to continued efforts the utilisation of already disbursed funds is showing encouraging trends in as much as 76% of funds released have reportedly been utilised.

The Corporation has launched a special scheme for eligible women beneficiaries of backward classes under the name of 'SWARNIMA'. The women beneficiaries get financial assistance at concessional rate of interest upto Rs. 1.00 lakh under the scheme. The Corporation has directed the SCAs to ensure 30% coverage of women beneficiaries under NBCFDC schemes out of which 5% will be covered under 'SWARNIMA' scheme. Effective steps are being taken to achieve this coverage.

New schemes for the welfare of the OBCs under implementation in ninth plan

The following Schemes have been launched in the year 1998-99 for the welfare of OBCs by the Government of India:-

Pre-examination coaching

The objective of the scheme is to coach/train candidates belonging to Other Backward Classes (OBCs) to enable them to compete on equal terms in various competitive/ entrance examinations covering. Recruitment to various services under the Central and State Governments, Public and Private Sector Undertakings Banks, GIC, LIC etc. and Defence Forces, State and Central Police Forces and Para-Military Forces and admission to technical, vocational, engineering medical, agricultural management courses etc. The candidates whose parents' or guardians total income from all sources including the income of the candidates is below Rs. 1.00 lakh annually will be eligible for admission in the pre-examination coaching centre under the scheme. An outlay of Rs. 2.00 crores have been provided for the scheme in 1998-99.

Hostel for OBC boys and girls

The scheme aims at providing better education opportunities to students belonging to socially and educationally backward classes notified as such in the Central/State/UT admn. list of OBC, generally referred to as Other Backward Classes (OBCs). It would, however, not cover students belonging to the Creamy Layer as defined in the Government of India, Ministry of Personnel, Public Grievances and Pensions (Department of Personnel and Training) OM No. 36012/22/93-Estt. (SCT) dated 08-09-1993. The Hostels under the scheme will be constructed in States/UTs which have a large OBC population but inadequate hostelsfacilities. These hostels will be constructed for middle, secondary college and university level students. Out of the Hostels to be set up under this scheme at least one third will be exclusively for girls. Five percent of the total seats in these hostels shall be reserved for disabled students-

The organisations eligible for assistance shall be as follows:-

(i) The State Governments and UTs concerned;

(ii) Institutions or organisations set up by the Government as autonomous body under statute or as a society under the Registration of Societies Act, 1860 or otherwise;

(iii) Educational and other institutions owned and controlled by either Central Government or State Government/UTs.

Under the scheme, 50% central assistance will be given for construction in such ewes The remaining 50% of the construction cost will have to be borne by the concerned State Government. Under the scheme 100% Central assistance will be given to the Central Government institutions and UTs proposing to set up such hostels. The entire expenditure on procurement of land, staffing and other maintenance and day to day expenditure shall be borne by the State Govt./ UT concerned. An outlay of Rs. 2.00 crores has been provided for the scheme in 1998-99.

Pre-matric scholarship for OBCS

Under this scheme, scholarship award will be sanctioned in the case of students whose parents/ guardians; income from all sources does not exceed Rs. 44,500 per annum. The scholarships are to be given to the students in class I or any subsequent class of pre-matric stage in the case of day scholars and class 11 or any subsequent class of pre-matric stage in the case of hostelers. The scholarship will terminate at the end of class X. The duration of scholarship in an academic year will be 10 months. The scholarship will be tenable in such institutions and for such pre-matriculation courses which have been duty recognised by the concerned State Government and Union territories Admn. 50% Central Assistance will be provided to the state Government under the scheme. An outlay of Rs. 2.00 crores; has been provided for the scheme in 1998-99.

Post-matric scholarships to the OBC students for studies In India

The objective of the scheme is to provide financial assistance to the OBC students studying at post-matriculation or post secondary stage to enable them to complete their education. These scholarship shall be available for' studies in India only and will be awarded by the Government of State/UT to which the applicant actually belongs, i.e. permanently settled 100% central assistance will be provided to State Governments/UT Admns for this purpose. The Central scholarships will be open to Indian nationals belonging to OBC as notified by the Central/State Government/UT Adrnn. These scholarships will be given for study in recognised institutions. Unemployed students whose parents/ guardians' income from all sources does not exceed Rs. 44,500.00 per annum will be entitled for scholarship under the scheme. An outlay of Rs. 5.00 cores has been provided for the scheme in 1998-99.

Assistance to voluntary organizations for welfare of OBCs

The aim of the scheme is to involve the voluntary sector to improve educational and socio-economic conditions of the target group i.e.. OBCs through skill upgradation and enable them to start income generating activities on their own or get gainfully employed. Assistance under the scheme will be admissible for establishing centres and developing services which may equip the OBCs by upgrading their skill to enable them to start income generating activities. The quantum of assistance is determined in each case on merit. The Government of India may, however, meet 90% of the approved expenditure on any or all of the specified items under the scheme. An outlay of Rs. 2.00 crores has been provided for the scheme in 1998-99.

7

Welfare of Minorities

The Constitution of India protects the interest of minorities both religious and linguistic and recognises their rights to conserve their language, script or culture and establish and administer educational institutions of their choice vide Article 29 and 30 of the Constitution. The Constitution also provides right to freedom of religion and freedom to manage religions affairs Article 350-A provides for instructions in the mother tongue at the primary stage of education to children belonging to linguistic minorities. Article 350-B provides for a Special Officer to investigate all matters relating to the safeguards provided for linguistic minorities under the Constitution.

Government has notified 5 communities namely Muslims, Sikhs, Christians, Buddhists and Zoroastrians as Minorities for the purposes of National Commission of Minorities Act, 1992. As per 1991 Census population of minority groups constitute 17.17% of the total population of the country.

15-Point programme for welfare of minorities

15 Point Programme for welfare of minorities classifies measures broadly under three categories namely, safety and protection of life and property, representation in the jobs under State and Central Governments and socio-

educational development. The programme envisages special consideration for minorities in recruitment and fair and adequate share in development programmes. The programme is being implemented by States/UTs and the concerned Central Ministries /Departments.

Monitoring of hte 15 point programme

The Ministry obtains reports in respect of Points 1 to 8 from the Ministry of Home Affairs. Half-yearly Reports in respect of Points 11 to 14 are obtained from the State. Governments /Departments. The information received from concerned agencies is compiled, analysed, reviewed and the deficiencies noticed in the implementation of the Programme are brought to the notice of the authorities concerned for remedial action. At the State level, the progress under the Programme is monitored at the level of Chief Minister/Chief Secretary. At the District level the Programme is monitored by Deputy Commissioner/ District Magistrate.

Recasting & updating of 15 point programme

The 15 Point Programme for the welfare of Minorities drawn up in 1983 is being recast so as to make it an effective instrument for ensuring nondiscrimination against the minorities and to focus on the positive steps required of be taken to create a feeling of confidence amongst them. The recasting of the 15 Point Programme is under active consideration of the Government of India.

Concerete measures taken by the concerned ministries/ departments

Ministry of Home Affairs has set up a Rapid Action Force charged with the special task of quelling communal riots. Guidelines have been issued to the State Governments on the measures for prevention of riots, dealing with situation arising out of riots and providing relief and rehabilitation to the riot victims. The guidelines for promotion of communal harmony, issued to State Governments in October, 1997 by Ministry of Home Affairs, included enhancement of the amount of ex-gratia in case of death or permanent incapacitation. There is a provision for assistance to the children of families affected by communal violence under National Foundation for Communal Harmony set up under the Ministry of Home Affairs which includes educational and vocational training to these children. According to the information received by the Home Ministry from different States/UTs, 8 States and one Union territory have constituted Special Courts specifically for communal offences. The total number of such Courts constituted so far are 22.

All India Radio and Doordarshan have been playing a major role in restoring communal harmony and peace in areas affected by communal riots. A communal harmony programme entitled "Bhagwan Se Poochun Ya Khuda Se" has been telecast on Prime Time every Sunday by Doordarshan and two current affairs programme highlighting economic development and Government efforts to promote the economic conditions of the minority communities in the North-East are regularly telecast on National Network of Doordarshan. All India Radio broadcasts a number of programmes on national integration and communal harmony through various stations across the country.

The Department of Education, Ministry of Human Resource Development started programmes of educational development in 41 identified districts; in the country with minority concentration. An Area Intensive Programme is being implemented at the block level of these 41 identified districts to provide basic educational infrastructure and facilities under this scheme 100% assistance is given by the Central Government.

Department of Education has introduced a Scheme to provide financial assistance for modernisation of Madras Education and for teaching of Science, Mathematics, Social Studies and Languages in traditional educational institutions (Madarsas/ Maktabs) on a voluntary basis. Under this Scheme 100% grant is given by the Central Government.

The 41 Minority concentration districts are also covered under the Scheme of Community Polytechnics to impart technical skills to eligible persons belonging to Minority communities. The enhancement of existing 41 minority concentration districts is under active consideration of Government

According to the information available from the States, 2965 trainees belonging to Minorities were trained in the ITIs from the year 1982-83 to 1996-97. Director General, Employment & Training Ministry of Labour also issued instructions to State Governments to ensure that there is no discrimination in matters of registration and sponsoring of minority candidates for vocational training courses.

Ministry of Social Justice & Empowerment set up an apex financial Corporation namely, National Minorities Development & Finance Corporation (NMDFC) with an authorised capital of Rs. 500 crores for providing concessional finance to eligible beneficiaries belonging to minorities for setting up self-employment ventures. Government of India's contribution to the equity capital of NMDFC was restricted to 25% of the paid up share capital. The balance will be held by the State Governments/

Corporations and individuals. During VIII Plan Rs. 125 crores have been released to the Corporation. The Government of India have raised the level of its contribution from Rs. 125.00 crores to Rs. 300.00 crores during the year 1998-99 subject to pro-rata contribution from the State Governments/UT Admns. towards the share capital of the Corporation. During the financial year 1998-99, (till February, 1999), the Corporation disbursed Rs. 30.92 crores as loan covering 6900 beneficiaries. The cumulative assistance provided by the Corporation since 199495 amounts to Rs. 134.85 crores for 36,899 beneficiaries.

National Minorities Development and Finance Corporation's share capital allocation and contribution by Government of India, year-wise sanctions/assistance and year-wise beneficiaries assisted may be seen at charts/graphs.

Department of Personnel and Training has issued instructions making it mandatory for all recruiting authorities of Central Government and PSUs to have one member belonging to minority community in the Selection Boards/Committees constituted for, making recruitment to 10 or more vacancies in Group 'C' and 'D' posts/services. Those sections of minorities which have been included in OBC list are eligible to take advantages of reservation provisions in the Civil Services and Posts under government of India at par with other OBC candidates.

Ministry of Social Justice & Empowerment has been operating a Scheme of Pre-Examination Coaching for Weaker Sections based on Economic Criteria among Minorities and other backward classes to enable them to compete on equal terms with other candidates in competitive examinations for various jobs. The Scheme is being implemented through institutions of repute. Rs. 3.65 crores have been released during VIIIth Five year Plan for this purpose. Since its inception in 1992-93 till 1997-98 the Scheme has covered 228 institutions while 10,840 candidates have been coached for various competitive examinations. During this financial year, i.e., 1998-99 (till February, 1999) Rs. 1.22 crores have been released under this Scheme. A similar Scheme is being implemented by University Grants Commission in 21 Universities and 32 colleges.

In pursuance of the strategy of area based approach for tackling the aproblems of minorities, the scheme of multi-sectoral development plans has been launched during 1995-96 in 41 minorities concentration districts. Under this Scheme, the concerned States are required to undertake surveys and prepare project reports through an expert agency in respect of activities conspicuously persued by the minorities in these districts with a view to identify the requirements of credit, marketing, training, technological support etc. for carrying out such activities in a viable way for development and welfare of minorities. An amount of Rs. 18.85 lakhs was disbursed during 1997-98 to the State Governments of Uttar Pradesh, Karnataka and Haryana. For 1998-99, an amount of Rs. 6.00 crores has been allocated for the Scheme. An itmount of Rs. 23.00 lakhs has been released to the State Governments of Uttar Pradesh and Gujarat under the Scheme during 1998-99.

National commission for minorities

In May, 1992, the National Commission for Minorities Act, 1992, was enacted giving statutory status to the erstwhile Minorities Commission and thus making it a more effective body to safeguard the interests of minorities. The National Commission for Minorities has been reconstituted w.e.f. 26.11.1996.

That National Commission for Minorities has so far submitted its 1st, 2nd, 3rd, 4th and 5th Annual Reports for placing the same before both the Houses of Parliament. Their recommendations are being examined in consultation with other Ministries/Departments. The National Commission for Minorities have constituted a High Powered Study Committee in June, 1997 to undertake a comprehensive study exclusively for the problems being faced by the major religious minorities in the country.

The National Commission for Minorities have also constituted a Minority Education cell to exclusively look after the problems being faced by Minority educational institutions in regard to recognition, affiliation, grants-in-aid etc.

Special officer for linguistic minorities

The Office of the Special Officer for Linguistic Minorities (commonly known as the Commissioner for Linguistic Minorities) was created in July, 1957, in pursuance of the provision of Article 350-B of the Constitution, which came into existence as a result of the recommendations of the State Reorganisation Commission. Under the said Article, it shall be the duty of the Commissioner for Linguistic Minorities to investigate all matters relating to the safeguards provided for the Linguistic Minorities under the Constitution and report to the President upon these matters at such intervals as the President may direct.

The Commissioner for Linguistic Minorities submits Annual Reports to the President of India. The Commissioner has so far submitted 34 Annual Reports, out of which 33 Annual reports have been tabled in Parliament.

The organisation of the Special officer for Linguistic Minorities has its headquarters at Allahabad with Regional offices at Calcutta, Belgaum and Madras. The Commissioner for Linguistic Minorities is assisted by a Deputy Commissioner, 4 Asstt Commissioners for

Linguistic Minorities and other officers and staff. Dr. Harbhajan Singh Deol has been appointed as Commissioner for Linguistic Minorities on 7.10.96

The Office of the Commissioner for Linguistic Minorities has been provided a budget allocation of Rs. 60.00 lakhs for 1998-99.

8

Youth Programmes

Youth represent the most vibrant section of the society They play a vital role with regard to socio-economic change as well as towards development of the society A nation can progress only when capabilities and energies of young people are canalised into constructive work. It is imperative that youth should have a major role in process of development. In India, youth forms nearly one-third- of the total population. With the objective of fulfilling the aspirations of this group and also empowering them to become active and constructive forces of positive change, the Department has been implementing several programmes.

National youth policy

The current National Youth Policy was evolved and tabled in the Parliament in November-December, 1988. The main objectives of the current Youth Policy are to instil in the youth respect for the principles and values enshrined in our Constitution; to promote among the youth an awareness of our historical heritage; to help develop in them the qualities of discipline, self-reliance, justice and fairplay; and to provide the youth with maximum access to education in addition to developing their personality It also aims at making the youth conscious of international issues and involving them in promoting world peace and a just international economic order.

A need was, however, felt for a new National Youth Policy geared not only to the fast changing socio-economic scenario in the country but also to address the future concerns of the youth. The Department accordingly drafted a new national Youth Policy which was circulated to all State Governments, Central Ministries/Departments, Universities, Youth Wings of Political Parties and Voluntary Organisations working in field of youth concerns for their comments. Based on the views received, a Draft New National Youth Policy has been prepared and is under consideration of the Government.

The salient features of the draft New Youth policy

The draft new National Youth Policy recognises that youth development is a multisectoral concept and calls for an integrated approach. It also stresses that the youth should be given more access to the process of decision making and implementation. It also defines privileges and responsibilities of youth.

Some important objectives of the Policy are to provide the youth with proper educational and employment opportunities; to give access to all relevant information; create adequate sports and other recreational facilities; to create among the youth awareness about Indian history, culture and heritage and to inculcate a scientific temper in them. The draft policy has set out four thrust areas viz., Youth Empowerment, Gender Justice, Intersectoral Approach and an Information and Research Network.

The Policy recognises the key sectors of concern for youth, such as Education, Training and Employment, Health and accords high priority to certain categories of youth . Such as, youth with disabilities, rural youth, unemployed youth and street children etc. Besides Education, Employment, and Health, the Policy also focuses on Adolescent Health, AIDS and Sexually Transmitted Diseases, Nutrition, Environment, Sports, Recreation and Leisure, Art and Culture, Gender Justice, Science and Technology, Civics and Citizenship.

National service scheme

National Service Scheme, popularly known as NSS, was launched in Gandhiji's Birth Centenary Year 1969, in 37 universities involving 40,000 students with primary focus on the development of personality of students through community service. Today, NSS has about 15 lakh student volunteers on its rolls spread over 189 universities, and senior secondary schools. From its inception, more than 1.52 crore students from the Universities, Colleges and Institutions of higher learning have benefited from NSS activities as NSS volunteers. Due to its overwhelming popularity and demand, the scheme was extended to the students of +2 level in selected institutions.

The National Service Scheme has two types of programmes, viz. "Regular Activities" and "Special Camping Programme" undertaken by its volunteers. Under 'Regular Activities', students are expected to work as volunteers for a continuous period of two years, rendering community service for minimum of 120 hours per annum. The activities include constructive work in adopted villages and slums, blood donation, adult and non-formal education, health, nutrition, family welfare, AIDS awareness campaigns, tree plantation, improvement of campuses, etc. Under "Special Camping Programme", a camp of 10 days' duration is conducted every year in the adopted areas on a specific theme like "Youth for Afforestation and Tree Plantation", "Youth for Rural Reconstruction", "Youth for Development", "Youth for Mass Literacy". " Youth for Social Harmony", etc.

The expenditure on programmes of NSS is shared between the Centre and the State Governments in the ratio of 7:5, except in the case of Jammu & Kashmir and Union Territories without Legislature, where the entire expenditure is met by the Central Government. The Central Government also meets the entire expenditure on administration, training, research, monitoring, evaluation and publications pertaining to the Scheme and the complete cost of NSS State Liaison Cells set up in the concerned Departments of State Governments. The existing pattern of expenditure on NSS Regular Activities and Special Camping Programme is Rs.120/- and Rs. 200/- per volunteer per annum respectively.

At the national level, Department of Youth Affairs & Sports in the Ministry of Human Resource Development, formulates the policy and programme guidelines for this scheme. National Service Scheme, which is a subordinate organisation under the Department is operating with 15 Regional Centres located at Ahmedabad, Bangalore, Bhopal, Bhubaneshwar, Calcutta Chandigarh, Guwahati, Hyderabad, Jaipur, Lucknow, Chennai, Patna, Pune and Tiruvananthpuram. In the Department, there is a Programme Adviser to advise the Government of India on matters pertaining to NSS Programme development.

For providing training, research and evaluation of the scheme and to motivate and equip the NSS functionaries with requisite skills, 4 Training Orientation and Research Centres (TORCs) and 14 Training and Orientation Centres (TOCs) have been set up. The Department meets the entire expenditure on maintenance of these TORCs and TOCs.

An AIDS awareness programme for students called "University Talk AIDS" has been introduced and has become very popular due to the peer educators concept adopted.

Indira Gandhi NSS Awards were introduced in 1994 to provide incentives to NSS functionaries and volunteers in order to give boost to the NSS programme.

Nehru Yuva Kendra Sangathan

Nehru Yuva Kendra Sangathan (NYKS) is an autonomous organisation of the Department of Youth Affairs & Sports. NYKS has its district level offices in about 500 districts of the country.

Over the year, NYKS has become the largest grassroots level organisation in Asia Pacific Region, catering to the needs of more than 6.4 million rural female and male youth enrolled through 1.79 lakh village-based organisations, named Youth Clubs, in the areas covering education, training, health awareness, self employment, financial assistance, etc. Besides this, awareness generation and activities for the overall development of the rural communities are also being taken up in the villages with emphasis on value, vision and voluntary action. Consequently, NYKS has emerged not merely as an organisation but as a movement.

For the implementation of the above programmes, every district NYKS has a network of trained cadre of District Youth Coordinators, National Service Volunteers and Youth Leaders. The strength of NYKS is its vast network of Youth Clubs at grassroots level.

Regular programmes of NYKS

Youth club development programme

To promote and develop Youth Club movement in the country so that the youth in the long run not only become self-reliant but also act as the catalytic agent in national development, NYKS organised 676 Youth Club Development Programmes during 1998-99.

Vocational training programme

To update and improve the vocational skills of the rural

youth to supplement their income. NYKS organised 2,550 Vocational Training Programmes.

Awareness campaign

This programme has been designed to use NYKS infrastructure to address the problems or issues of local and national importance affecting the life of people particularly the youth of rural areas. NYKS organised 3467 such camps during the year.

Work camp

In order to promote the spirit of self-help, creation and sustenance of community values and assets, to inculcate a feeling of dignity of labour, to involve youth club members in project planning and management and to improve the organisational skills of Youth Club members, NYKS organised 894 Work Camps.

Celebration of National Youth day and youth week

All NYKs in the country celebrated National Youth Day on January 12 and National Week from January 12 to 19. A total of 6,759 such programmes were **organised by NYKS to propagate** the ideals of great men for community welfare and national development.

Sports promotion programmes

To lay focussed attention on the development of rural sports scenario and also to inculcate sports culture in rural areas, NYKS organised 1,272 Sports Promotion Programmes.

Cultural programmes

In order to preserve and enrich the cultural heritage of the country as well as to disseminate important messages of different issues of national and international importance through the media of Folk Art and Culture; NYKS organised 1498 cultural Programmes. These programmes were organised in the form of Folk Dances, Folk Songs, Folk Skits, Nukkad Nataks, Plays, Puppetry, etc.

Programmes in collaboration with other agencies

"Youth Action Goal - 2000 : Health for all, Education for all"

NYKS in Uttar Pradesh in collaboration with UNICEF has taken up a programme called "youth action goal-2000", which has five major components, known as "Panch Parameshwar", namely, Child Education, Health and Immunization, Drinking Water, Nutrition & Family Welfare. Out of the 12,625 village panchayats in Uttar Pradesh the Panch Parmeshwar Programme is being implemented in 9,000 village panchayats

The trained field functionaries have undertaken activities ranging from block level campaigns, sanitation awareness drives and cultural programmes to development of local level education centres for literacy and self-employment etc.

Mahila samriddhi yojana

NYKS in collaboration with the Department of Women and Child Development, Government of India is implementing a project entitled Mahila Samriddhi Yojana in 40 districts of the country. In each district, 4 clusters of 25 villages where NYKS have active Youth Clubs, are selected (making a total of 100 villages). Therefore, under this project, 8000 young women hailing from 4000 villages are imparted training so that they, at their level, can take up this programme on voluntary basis.

Youth against AIDS campaign in north-eastern states

NYKS in collaboration with National AIDS Control Organisation (NACO) has taken up this project in 45 districts of North-Eastern States. In the first phase of the project after selection of the vulnerable districts, Youth Coordinators are imparted 5 day Master's Training Programme so that they not only act as the trainers of the trainees but also can implement the project at their own level. In order to develop a second line leadership of trainers, 2765 Youth leaders from all the blocks are imparted training, in the field of HIV-AIDS.

Through a programme, called AIDS Education Block Level Campaign (AEBLC) following steps are being taken :

(a) Formation of Districts AIDS Control Committee in every district.

(b) Formation of Folk Media teams.

(c) Formation of 12 members campaign team from a corpus of 27 persons.

(d) Listing of the nodal villages and formation of itinerary for the campaign teams.

Health awareness units projects

NYKS in collaboration with Ministry of Health & Family Welfare has taken up a project entitled Health Awareness Units for implementation in 135 districts of the country. The total cost of the project is Rs.2.40' crores, over a period of three years.

The principal objective of the project is to generate awareness, educate, motivate and popularize Health & Family Welfare programmes through active cooperation and participation of local Youth Clubs and Mahila Mandals affiliated with district Nehru Yuva Kendra and people in general.

Awareness on child rights

NYKs in Rajasthan are implementing Child Rights project in collaboration with Rajasthan unit of UNICEF. In the first phase of this project, 30 Youth Coordinators of Rajasthan are being imparted orientation training in the form of a workshop which is followed by imparting three day training to 240 NSVs.

Project on awareness generation cum management of water resource through youth

Nehru Yuva Kendra Sanganthan in co-ordination with the Ministry of Water Resources, Government of India has taken up a Project entitled 'Awareness Generation -cum Management of Water Resources' through youth. The principal objective of this project is to study water management system and practices in villages and to suggest as well as to undertake improvements therein.

'North-eastern school students cultural exchange programme

Nehru Yuva Kendra Sangathan in co-ordination with Ministry of Home Affairs has undertaken a project entitled 'North -Eastern Students Cultural Exchange Programme".

The main objective of this project is to provide an opportunity to school students of the North East to see different places of cultural interest in the country. This will also encourage the youth of North-Eastern region to make friends with people belonging to the other areas of the' country and to continue this friendship over the years. During the period under report, six such Cultural Exchange Programmes, involving 250 students of North- - East, were organised

Implementation of DYAS scheme

NYKS also implements following schemes of Department of Youth Affairs & Sports

(1) Youth Development Centres

(2) Scheme for Financial Assistance to Youth Clubs.

(3) National Service Volunteers Scheme.

National service volunteer scheme

The National Service Volunteer Scheme, launched in 1977-78, aims at providing opportunities to youth to involve themselves, on a voluntary basis, in nation building activities for a year or two. Any person who has completed his/her degree course and is below 25 years of age may get himself/herself enrolled as a National Service Volunteer (NSV) for one/two years. The requirement of age and educational qualification can be relaxed in case of SC/ST and women volunteers. Each volunteer is paid a stipend of Rs.500/-per month and a fixed travelling allowance @ Rs.200/-per month. They are also given a contingency grant of Rs.100/- per year.

At present, 8500 NSVs are deployed with the Nehru Yuva Kendra Sangathan, National Service Scheme, Bharat Scouts & Guides, Youth Hostels Association of India, etc. The State Governments/Union Territories are also availing of the services of these volunteers.

Assistance to voluntary organisations in the field of youth

The scheme provides financial assistance to voluntary organisations to involve youth for developmental activities, specially in the rural areas. Under the scheme, assistance is extended to registered bodies, public trusts and non-profit making companies.

The main focus of this scheme has been on vocational training programme to promote self-employment for youth. Assistance is also given for conducting youth leadership training programme to promote cadres of young dynamic persons who would act as catalysts of social change in the rural areas. During the financial year 199899,up to 1.3.99 an amount of Rs.138.00 lakhs has been released to 110 voluntary organisations, for benefiting 3345 persons.

Training of youth

The Scheme aims at improving the productive potential of youth through training ,courses based on local needs and talent for promoting self-employment and better employment. It is being implemented through the voluntary organisations, Nehru Yuva

Kendras, NSS Regional Centres, educational institutions and State Governments/UT Administrations, The training covers a wide range of disciplines like agriculture, animal husbandry, dairy, poultry, etc. Other training programmes aimed at uplifting the functional capabilities of the rural youth and preparing them for self-employment are encouraged.

During the financial year 1998-99 (up to 1.3.99) , an amount of Rs.120. lakh was released to 67 voluntary organisations for training 3855 youth.

Special scheme for promotion of youth activities among the youth of backward tribes

In order to promote youth activities among the youth of backward tribes based on their need and potential, this special scheme was started during 1990-91. Under the Scheme, Central Assistance is given to voluntary organisations, National Service Scheme Regional Centres, Educational institutions including Universities, Nehru Yuva Kendras, Bharat Scouts and Guides and also to State Government/Union Territory administrations for conducting youth leadership training programmes, vocational training for self-employment; and programming on general awareness according to the norms prescribed for simelar scheme for general category youth in the various ongoing youth welfare schemes.

During the financial year 1998-99 (up to 1.3-99) an amount of Rs.98.93 lakhs has been released for 81 voluntary organisations for 8075 youth.

Exhibitions for youth

The Scheme of Exhibitions for Youth aims at:-

i) projecting and recognising the activities and contribution made by youth in various fields of national development

ii) promoting the spirit of secularism and national integration,

iii) enabling youth to know more about the ways of life and culture of other parts of the country.

Exhibitions on folk dances, folk songs, painting, art and crafts, books, as well as on various development and youth related schemes are covered under this scheme.

Financial assistance is given to voluntary organisations, NYK Sangathan, NSS Regional Centres, educational institutions including Universities, State Governments/ U.T.s. The Department of Youth Affairs and Sports itself organizes such exhibitions also.

During the financial year 1998-99 an amount of Rs.13.59 lakhs was released for organising 18 exhibitions.

Rajiv Gandhi national institute of youth development

The Rajiv Gandhi National Institute of Youth Development has been set up at Sriperumbudur (Tamil Nadu). The Institute functions as an autonomous body registered under the Societies Registration Act. Its objectives are training, documentation, research and evaluation and extension work on all youth related activities in the country. The Institute will also:

— function as a research agency and think-tank for youth programmes, policies and implementation strategies;

— develop multi -faceted programmes for youth; function as an institute for advanced studies in the field of youth;

— function as a Centre for documentation, information and publication pertaining to youth development; and

— work as a Resource Centre.

The construction of the 1 st and 2nd phases of its building is likely to be completed during current financial year For the financial year 1998-99, a budget provision of Rs.505.00 lakhs has been provided.

Programmes conducted

1. One day workshop on Youth Related issues for the student youth was held on 15-10-98 in collaboration with University of Madras.

2. A Training Programme on "Youth Entrepreneurship and Economic Development" for youth functionaries with CYP Asia Centre, Chandigarh was held from 7-12th December, 1998. 30 participants from Government and non Government organisations attended the training programme.

3. A trainers, programme for the Development Management Practitioners on "Developmental Challenges in the 21st century" was organised from 23-28th December, 1998 at Xavier Institute of Management, Bhubaneswar in collaboration with CYP Asia Centre.

4. In pursuance of the agreement made with the UNESCO for the preparation of CD-ROM on youth profile, Heads of Institutions from the TORCs were invited on 25.1.99 for a meeting and to give their proposal for the collection/ compilation of data on youth profile in their region.

5. A programme on "Environmental Youth Services Programme" for 30 unemployed youth and school dropouts from Chennai City was conducted in collaboration with EXNORA International in January, 1999.

6. A one day seminar on "Human Rights & Democracy - Youth Perspective" was organised on 24th February, 1999.

7. CYP Asia Centre has proposed to organise in collaboration with RAGNIYD the Commonwealth Day Celebrations on 8th March, 1999 at Chennai.

Scouting and guiding

Scouting & Guiding is an educational and international movement aiming at developing the character of boys and girls, making them develop as good citizens of the country and inculcating in them a spirit of patriotism, sympathy for others and social service. Scouting and Guiding also promotes balanced physical and mental development.

The organisation, mainly promoting these activities in India, is Bharat Scouts and Guides to which the Department extends financial assistance both towards administrative expenditure and activities viz. training camps, skills, developing & holding of jamborees. It is the one of the largest youth organisations having 23 lakh enrolment and the third largest in the world with about 85,000 units spread all over the country. These units conduct their activities in the areas of adult literacy, tree plantation, community service, leprosy awareness, crafts' centres and promotion of hygiene and sanitation. Bharat Scouts & Guides is also associated with various programmes run by WHO and UNICEF in different fields. Financial assistance of Rs 89 lakh was given to the Bharat Scouts and Guides during 1998-99. The other organisation active in this field is All India Boy Scouts Association.

Promotion of adventure

This scheme aims at fostering in youth the spirit of risk-taking, endurance, cooperative team work and encouraging quick, ready and effective reflexes in challenging situations. Financial assistance is provided to institutions, groups, individuals and voluntary organisations for undertaking adventure activities. The number of activities covered under the scheme has been enlarged. During the current financial year, major thrust was on providing financial assistance for creation of infrastructure and promotion of Aero-sports & Water Sports. The Department provided assistance for 110 adventure programmes, involving on amount Rs. 120 lakh, during the year 1998-99 (upto 1.3.99)

Department provided financial assistance to important expeditions like

1. Solo Trans India Air Expeditions from Rajasthan to Arunachal Pradesh by Sqn. Ldr. B.K. Das & his team.
2. Milleniurn Everest Expedition 1999, to be undertaken by Ms Santosh Yadav and her team

Promotion of national integration

The Scheme for Promotion of National Integration aims at providing financial assistance for a variety of youth programmes aimed at fostering national integration and communal harmony. The scheme provides the framework for greater exchange and understanding among youth of the various regions of the country and for greater involvement of voluntary agencies in the task of national integration. Inter State Youth Exchange programmes are also arranged to facilitate visit of youth living and working in the border States to States with marked cultural difference and an exchange visit by youth of those States to the border States. The funds are canalized through a number of voluntary youth organisations. During 1998-99, 148 National Integration Camps for rural and urban youth and 7 inter-state youth exchange programmes were organised for which a financial assistance of Rs. 279 lakhs has been given upto 1.3.99.

National youth festival

The Fifth National Youth Festival jointly organised by Nehru Yuva Kendra Sangathan, Department of Youth Affairs & Sports, Government of India and Department of Youth Welfare and Prantiya Vikas Dal, Government of

U.P. was formally inaugurated by the Prime Minister of India, Shri Atal Behari Vajpayee on 12th January, 1999 at K.D. Singh Babu Stadium in Lucknow amidst a massive gathering of more than 30,000 people and school children. About 3500 youth from all over India participated in the function. Speaking on this occasion the Prime Minister called upon the youth to rise above the considerations of religion, region, language and caste and contribute towards the progress of the nation which is gearing for next millenium.

National youth award

On this occasion, the Prime Minister also conferred National Youth Awards along with scroll on the youth in recognition of their commendable services for community welfare and social development.

National youth convention

Nehru Yuva Kendra Sangathan and Department of Youth Affairs and Sports organised a National Youth Convention on 'Youth, Voluntary Service and Nation Building' on 14 January at Kisan Ganna Sansthan, Lucknow (U.R). This National Youth Convention was organised as a part of the Fifth National Youth Festival.

Social development fair and craft bazaar

A Social Development Fair and Craft Bazaar was organised by Nehru Yuva Kendra Sangathan and Department of Youth Affairs and Sports, Government of India at Begurn Hazrat Mahal Park in the premises of, K.D. Singh Babu Stadium, Lucknow (U.P) The Fair is an attempt to introduce common people to some of the National, International NGOs and Voluntary Agencies who have been pursuing the greater social and human cause relentlessly over several years.

Seminars

Two seminars were also organised during the festival on

"Youth and Employment , and "Youth as Agents of Development". These seminars were attended by NSS volunteers, youth representatives from NYKS and State Government representatives.

Youth hostels

Youth Hostels are built to promote youth travel to enable them the young people', experience the rich cultural heritage of our country. The construction of Youth Hostels has been conceived as a joint venture of the Central and State Governments. While,, the Central Government bears the cost of the construction, the State Government, provides developed land free of cost with water, electricity, approach roads and st quarters. Youth Hostels, after completion, are handed over to the State Government for management. Till date 56 Youth Hostels have been constructed and 18 more are under construction. The Youth Hostel is looked after by the Warden and Assistant Warden, a husband-wife team, and paid an honorarium of Rs.3000/- per month. During the financial year 1998-99, out of the budget provision of Rs. 300.00 lakh, Rs.217.00 lakh has been released for construction and furnishing of Youth Hostel buildings.

Assistance to youth clubs

With a view to give a new thrust to the youth movement in the country, the scheme' of Assistance to Youth Clubs was started by the Department in 1986-87. It is being[" implemented through NYK Sangathan and State Governments/Union Territory Administrations. It aims at assisting newly set up Youth Clubs at the grassroots level.

On the basis of recommendations of the Working Group constituted for the formulation of Ninth Five Year Plan, the Scheme of Assistance to Sports Clubs/Centres

has been merged with the Scheme of Assistance to Youth Clubs to make it more broad based and need based to be known as "Scheme of Assistance to Rural Youth and Sports Clubs".

During the financial year 1998-99 (up to 1.3.99), an amount of Rs.65.90 lakh was released to NYK Sangathan for further disbursement to 1318 Youth Clubs.

Scheme of youth development centres

In order to promote participation of rural youth in development activities, a new scheme for setting up of Youth Development Centres for a group of 10 villages each was introduced during 1994-95. However, initially each centre may cover more than 10 villages. The centres are responsible for creation of facilities for information, sports, training and youth programmes for rural youth. The land for the centre is to be donated by the Panchayat.

One time financial assistance of not more than Rs. 30,000/- is given to each Centre to cater to the requirements of furniture, equipment, radio and TVNCP. Each centre is to be managed by a Youth Committee drawn from the youth of the constituent villages. The operation and maintenance expenses are to be raised by the Committee. This Scheme is being implemented through the NYK Sangathan.

During the financial year 1998-99, an amount of Rs.33.60 lakh was released to NYK Sangathan for further disbursement to 112 Youth Development Centres.

Award to outstanding youth clubs

With a view to recognising the contribution of youth clubs and motivating them for more active participation in the nation-building endeavour, this scheme was introduced during 1992-93. It is being implemented through the Nehru Yuva Kendra Sangathan. The scheme operates on a three-tier basis, i.e. District, State and National levels. At the district level the winner receives an award of Rs.5,000/- and at the State level Rs.20,000/. At the national level, there are three awards of Rs.1.00 lakh, Rs.50,000/- and Rs.25,000/-. The prize money is to be used for implementation of more community based projects.

9

Sports and Physical Education

India has a long tradition of sports and physical fitness. There are several references to excellence in Archery, Wrestling and other sports in the Ramayana, the Mahabharat and ancient writings. After Independence, the importance of sports was formally recognized with the holding of the 9th Asian Games in Delhi in 1982. A separate Department was created in 1982. The first National Sports Policy was announced in 1984.

During the year 1998-99, Shri Sachin Tendulkar was awarded the prestigious Rajiv Gandhi Khel Ratna Award for the year 1997-98. Besides, Arjuna Awards for the year 1997 were presented to 21 outstanding sportspersons at Rashtrapati Bhawan on 29th August 1998. The revised draft new Sports Policy was discussed in different meetings/fora and views expressed therein were considered. The Policy is under finalisation.

Sports authority of India

The Sports Authority of India (SAI) which is a successor organization of the Special Organizing Committee (SOC) for the IX Asian Games held in Delhi in 1982 was set up in 1984 by the Government of India with the objective of maintaining and utilizing the stadia created /renovated for the 1982 Asian Games and to spot and nurture talented children under different sports promotion schemes to achieve excellence at national/international levels.

SAI through its Regional Centres located at Bangalore, Gandhinagar, Delhi, Chandigarh, Calcutta and Imphal and Sub-centre at Guwahati is implementing various sports promotion schemes. The Regional Centres are equipped with sports science back-up and also provide conducive atmosphere ' and facilities for training of budding talent. Apart from these Regional Centres, SAI has Academic Wings at NSNIS Patiala and LNCPE, Thiruvananthapuram. SAI also has a High Altitude Training Centre (HATC) at Shillaroo (HP).

The different sports promotion schemes of SAI which were conceived and formulated during VII Five Year Plan for development and promotion of sports at grassroots level in the country were reviewed at different fora from time to time. These schemes were last reviewed by the SAI Governing Body at its meeting held on 16.10.98. The Governing Body recommended that while SAI should consolidate its existing schemes, it should establish one Centre for Excellence in each Regional Centre for girls. These efforts would generate more input of talent and identify the appropriate persons for being trained to achieve excellence in sports at national and international levels.

National Sports Talent Contest (NSTC) scheme

The scheme aims at selecting school children in the age group of 8-12 years through a battery of tests in Athletics, Badminton, Basketball, Football, Gymnastics, Hockey, Swimming, Table Tennis, Wrestling and Volleyball for their scientific training in the SAI Adopted Schools. At present 29 schools (including 8 day boarding) and two Akharas with 1021 trainees are functioning throughout the country.

Adoption of akharas for promotion of wrestling

In order to tap the rural youth who still continue to be trained in conventional Akharas, there is a scheme for adoption of Akharas. Under the scheme, boys under 14 years of age who have already shown prominence in wrestling during training in the Akharas, are adopted by SAI and to meet their diet & school expenses, a stipend is given to them. At present following 2 Akharas in Maharashtra have been adopted under the scheme of NSTC:-

i) Krida Vikas Vyayam Mandal, Sangli -09 Wrestlers

ii) Gokul Ustad Tamil, Pune - 15 Wrestlers

Army Boys Sports Company (ABSC) Scheme

The scheme which is an extension of NSTC Scheme provides for scouting for talented boys in the age group of 8-12 years for admitting them into the Regimental Centres of the Army. Thereafter they are given training on scientific lines with due care for their regular education.

At present there are 16 ABSCs with 714 trainees.

Special Area Games (SAG) Scheme

The scheme envisages identification of the budding talent from tribal, rural & coastal areas of the country and from the regions which are genetically or physically gifted for achieving excellence in a particular discipline like Archery, Fencing, Athletics, Boxing, Weightlifting, Shooting, Wrestling, Hockey, Water Sports, Cycling, Judo, etc. Apart from this, talent is also tapped of those individuals who traditionally take- part in indigenous games and martial arts of the country~ The selected talented boys and girls are admitted in the SAG Centres for in house scientific training where educational and vocational training is also imparted to them. At present 9 SAG centres with 361 sportspersons (286 Boys 75 Girls) are being trained.

SAI training centres

Consequent to reviewing of the sports promotional schemes by the Governing Body, the Sports Hostel Scheme and the Sports Project Development Area (SPDA) Scheme stand merged as SAI Training Centres. These - centres cater to children in the age group of 14-21 years. At present 40 SAI Training centres spread all over the country are imparting training to 1713 (1579 boys & 134 girls) sportspersons.

National coaching scheme

Under this scheme, SAI coaches are provided to the State Government/UT Administrations on matching basis for State Coaching Centres and District Coaching Centres. SAI Coaches are also provided at SAI Stadia in Delhi to impart training to the trainees under Regular Coaching Scheme and also to the Wrestling Akharas and the National Academies of various disciplines. SAI coaches also impart training to the national campers and to SAI trainees under different sports promotion schemes in the field units, besides assisting the Academic wing in the conduct of Diploma and Master's Course in different coaching disciplines. A few SAI coaches are also posted in the Kendriya Vidayalayas and Navodaya Vidalayas and the Field Stations in some Universities.

Presently there are 1636 coaches on the rolls of SAL

Centre of excellence

Under this scheme talented sportpersons in the age group of 14-21 years from the SAI Scheme as well as the schemes being run by the State Governments. UTs are to be selected for scientific training in order to achieve excellence at the international level. To begin with, a Centre of Excellence for Hockey was set up in Bangalore in 1997.

Central pool of technical sports equipment

There is a Central Pool of Technical Sports Equipment at

Corporate office, New Delhi from which equipments are given on loan basis to Sports Federations, Departmental Undertakings, Educational Institutions, sports bodies and other organizations which are involved in the promotion of sports, for conducting sports tournaments. Equipment support was extended to various agencies during the year.

Medical centre

The Medical Centre at the Corporate Office is well equipped with medical and health facilities besides having proper sports science facilities and a Dope Control Laboratory to aid and advise the sportspersons at different levels and SAI Trainees under different sports tournaments at the national/international level. The medical coverage during the sports tournaments being held in SAI Stadia is also extended by SAI to the organizers of these tournaments.

Sports academics

Following Sports Academics have been set up by SAI in collaboration with the Public /Private Sector Undertakings in order to create an environment of sports consciousness in the country and also to ensure a continuous programme of development of excellence with adequate academic support, requisite nutrition and international exposure: -

i) National Academy for Hockey by Air India at National Stadium, New Delhi.

ii) National Academy for Handball at Bhilai/ Rourkela by SAIL.

iii) Regional Hockey Academy for Tribal Youth at Rourkela by SAIL.

iv) Tennis Academy by Central Excise at SAI Centre, Calcutta.

v) Archery Academy by Northern Coalfields Ltd. at Singrauli.

vi) Chess Academy by Goodricke at Calcutta.

vii) Table Tennis Academy by Petroleum Sports Control Board and Table Tennis Federation of India (TTFI) at Ajmer.

viii) Gymnastics Academy by Allahabad Gymnastics Association at Allahabad.

ix) Volleyball Academy by Vishakhapatnam Steel Plant at Vishakhapatnam.

Schemes of DYAS being implemented by SAI on agency basis

The following schemes of DYAS are being implemented by the Academic Wing of SAI located at Netaji Subhash National Institute Sports, (NS NIS) Patiala on agency basis:-

a) Sports Scholarship Scheme.

b) Rural Sports Programme

c) National Sports Festival for Women.

Sports science research fellowship scheme

Under this scheme 5-6 scholarships are offered annually to doctors and scientists and project grants are given to selected institutions to motivate and encourage them for research in the different components of sports science - nutrition, physiology, psychology and sports injuries.

Academic wings of SAI

The Academic Wing of SAI consists of Netaji Subash National Institute of Sports at Patiala and Lakshmibai National College of Physical Education, Thiruvananthapuram.

SAI-NS NIS-patiala

The duration of the Diploma course has been curtailed to one year with the approval of DYAS from the academic session of 1997-98. The Course is being conducted at Patiala and Bangalore in the following disciplines:-

	Patiala		*Bangalore*
1)	Athletics	1)	Archery
2)	Badminton	2)	Basketball
3)	Boxing	3)	Football
4)	Cycling	4)	Swimming
5)	Gymnasstics	5)	Volleyball
6)	Hockey		
7)	Judo		
8)	Table Tennis		
9)	Tennis		
10)	Wrestling		
11)	Weightlifting		

The DYAS has also approved the conduct of the following courses:-

Advanced course in coaching - This course is mainly meant for the coaches identified for the training of the national teams and will be conducted at Patiala for a period of 6 months for one discipline at a time.

Special Course in coaching for North East Region. - This course of one year duration is conducted exclusively for the students from North East region at SAI Eastern Centre, Calcutta in six disciplines, providing for relaxation in respect of the educational qualifications in view of the dearth of coaches in the North East.

1) Athletics
2) Badminton
3) Boxing

4) Hockey

5) Judo

6) Weightlifting

SAI - Lakshmibai National College of Physical Education Thiruvananthapuram (LNCPE)

This College is dedicated to the upliftment of Physical Education and Sports in the Country and serves as a model institute for Teachers, Training. Besides having excellent sports facilities, the college is equipped with a Sports Science Lab items, Library, Gymnastics Centre and a Velodrome.

A. The College offers the following Courses:-

i) 3-year Bachelor's Degree in Physical Education

ii) 2-year Master's Degree in Physical Education Students' Strength

	Boys	Girls	Total
BPE-I	29	20	49
BPE-II	30	20	50
BPE-III	26	17	43
MPE-I	20	5	25
MPE-II	9	13	22
	114	75	189

Preparation of national teams for major international sports events

The Sports Authority of India in collaboration with the National Sports Federations/ Association prepares the national teams for different sports tournaments at the international level.

Long Term Development Training Plans in respect of the targeted disciplines for the major international tournaments prepared by the respective national federation/ association are discussed and finalized by the SAI with the approval of the DYAS and technical support in terms of foreign coaches/experts, foreign exposure of the teams, facilities for coaching of the national teams and equipment including imported one are provided to the national campers/ players at the SAI Centres/Training venues.

The Commonwealth Games and Asian Games were the two mega sports events held during the year 1998 for which National Teams and sportpersons were imparted intensive coaching.

Sports protocols and cultural exchange programmes

The Sports Protocols and Cultural Exchange Programmes (CEPs) executed by the Government of India from time to time with the other countries are implemented by SAI. The protocols/CEPs generally envisage exchange of sportspersons, sports scientists, sports equipment, sports literature etc. on mutually agreed terms. During 1998-99, H.E. Mr. S. Thondaman, Minister for Livestock Development & Estate Infrastructure of Sri Lanka met Director General SAI on 23.1.99 and visited the Patiala & Bangalore Centres where he held discussions regarding training of Sri Lankan Physical Education Teachers/ Coaches at the Academic Wing of SAI. Consequently, 9 Sri Lankan Coaches have been enrolled for a refresher course in Athletics (5), Basketball (1), Football (1) & Volleyball (1) (6 at NSNIS Patiala & 2 at Bangalore).

India signed an MOU with Mauritius on 19.2.99 and another MOU with Australia on 26.2.99 for cooperation in the field of sports.

Utilisation of SAI stadia

The following stadia in Delhi which were created/ renovated during the IX Asian Games held in 1982 are being maintained and utilized by SAI for use by sportspersons, teams & for holding national/international events:-

i) Jawaharlal Nehru Stadium

ii) Indira GGandhi Stadium

iii) National Stadium

iv) Talkatora Swimming pool

v) Dr. Karni Singh Shooting Ranges

The sports facilities available in these stadia for different sports disciplines are being utilized under the Regular Coaching Scheme. Those not covered under this have the option to avail of facilities under the Pay & Play Scheme. The response from the trainees/sports lovers in the use of stadia has been quite encouraging. Apart from this, as and when required, the federations and other organizations both in the pubic and private sectors, and educational institutions utilize these facilities for conducting their sports tournaments/cultural programmes.

Work study by staff inspection unit (SIU)

The SIU conducted its study of SAI and as per the Final Report submitted by it to the Government, there are 487 posts surplus in different categories as per details given below :-

The SIU report has been accepted by SAI and is being considered by the Government.

Grants for promotion of games and sports in universities/ colleges

The Scheme of Grants for Promotion of Sports in Universities and Colleges, which was under revision has since been finalised and has come into force with effect from 22.6.98. Under this scheme, assistance is provided to the Universities/Colleges for development of playgrounds, construction of Indoor Stadia & other sports

S. No.	Category of the Post	Sanctioned Strenggth	Existing Strength	Assessed Agreed Strength	Surplus with reference to Workiing Strength
1.	A	252	183	170	13
2.	B	93	58	65	7
3.	C	796	662	525	137
4.	D	1415	1303	959	344
	Total :	2556	2206	1719	487

facilities in the ratio of 75:25 in the case of Special Category States and in the ratio of 50 : 50 to all other States, subject to certain ceilings. Assistance is also given for the purchase of sports equipment upto maximum ceiling of Rs. 3.00 lakh without any matching share from the Institutions. The Association of Indian Universities (AIU) is also provided assistance for holding Coaching/ Training Camps of Sportspersons, interuniversity tournaments and participation in foreign tournaments. Maulana Abul Kalam Azad Trophy, a rolling trophy, is also awarded every year to the overall winner of inter university tournaments. This year, the trophy was awarded to the Guru Nanak Dev University, Amritsar for winning 1st Position in the University tournaments of 199697. Cash incentives of Rs. 1.00 lakh, 50,000/- and Rs. 25,000/- are also given to the Universities winning the first three positions for the purchase of sports equipment.

During 1998-99, budget provision for this scheme was Rs. 3.09 crore which was subsequently revised to Rs.5.00 crore. Against this revised estimate, the actual expenditure was Rs.2.81 crore (as on 8.2.99). (Details of grants given under this Scheme can be seen at Annexure - III.)

Grants for creation of sports infrastructure

The Scheme of Grants for Creation of Sports

Infrastructure, which was under revision for the last 2-3 years, was finalised and is in operation since 1st September, 1998. Under this scheme, Grants are given to State Governments, UT Administrations, Local Statutory Bodies such as Municipalities, Municipal Corporations/ Notified Area Committees/Cantonment Boards and Registered Voluntary Organisations active in the field of sports. Grant can be availed of by them for Development of Playfields, Construction of Indoor/Outdoor Stadia, Swimming pool, Water Sports Infrastructure, Skating Rinks, Velodromes, Sports Hostels, Winter Sports Infrastructure, Shooting Ranges and Additional facilities in existing sports projects. In addition, State/UT Governments are also assisted for construction of District/State Level Sports complexes. Financial assistance is rendered subject to the cost being shared between the Union Government and the sponsoring agencies/State Government concerned in the ratio of 75:25 in respect of Special Category States, Hilly/Tribal Areas and 50:50 in case of other Areas. The Central Undertakings, Kendriya Vidalaya Sangathan and Navodaya Vidalaya Samiti will also be eligible to avail of the assistance for construction/ improvement of certain facilities in their schools.

During 1998-99, budget provision for this scheme was Rs. 11.60 crore, which was subsequently revised to Rs.4.00 crore. Against this revised estimate, the actual expenditure was Rs.2.10 crore (as on 8.2.99). State-wise details of the central assistance sanctioned during the last 3 years, including the current year, are given in Annexure - IV.

Grants to rural schools for sports equipment and playgrounds

This is a Sub-Scheme of the Main Scheme of Grants for Creation of Sports Infrastructure. This Scheme was also under revision and the revised provisions have come into force with effect from 1st April, 1998. Secondary/Senior Secondary Schools located in Rural Areas and fulfilling the conditions regarding availability of a playfield of a requisite size, having a regularly appointed Physical Education Teacher etc. are given grant up to a maximum of Rs.50 lakh for development of playfield and or purchase of consumable/non-consumable sports equipment. There is no matching contribution required against this grant either from the States/UT Governments or the school. Only one school per year per block and not exceeding two schools per block during a Plan Period, will be provided assistance under the scheme. Schools in the hilly areas have also been made eligible for grant towards fencing of playground.

During 1998-99 budget provision for this scheme was Rs.40.00 lakh which was subsequently revised to Rs.100.00 lakh. Against this revised estimate, the actual expenditure was Rs.39.00 lakh (As on 8.2.99).

Laying of synthetic track/artificial hockey and others surfaces

Under this revised scheme, which is effective from 1.9.98, State/UTs, State Sports Councils/Authorities, Sports Authority of India, National Sports Associations/ Federations, Services/Railway Sports Control Boards, Local bodies and University/Colleges/ Schools are provided central assistance. The assistance will also be made available to the Public/Private Sector Enterprises which are running Sports Academies and Sports Hostels for promoting sports excellence. Under the scheme, assistance upto Rs.1.00 crore or 50% of the estimated cost, whichever is less, is provided for laying or replacement of the hockey surface and athletic track only.

During 1998-99, budget provision for the scheme was Rs.5.50 crore, which was subsequently revised to Rs. 3.50 crore. Against this revised estimate, the actual expenditure was Rs.1.10 crore (as on 8.2.99).

Rajiv Gandhi Khel Ratna Award

The scheme was launched from the year 1991-92 with the objective of honouring sportspersons to enhance their general status and to give them greater dignity and place of honour in society. Under this scheme, an amount of Rs.1.00 lakh is given as award for the most spectacular and outstanding performance in the field of sports by an individual sportsperson or a team. Shri Sachin Tenclulkar was given Rajiv Gandhi Khel Ratna Award for the year 1997-98 for his outstanding achievements in the field of Cricket.

Cash awards to medal winners in international sports events

Special cash awards ranging from Rs. 50,000/- to Rs.5,00,000/- are given for winning medals in specified international sports events in disciplines which are included in the Olympic, Asian and Commonwealth Games. The award money ranging from Rs.50,000/- to 5,00,000/- is being enhanced from Rs. 5 lakh to 15 lakh shortly. These awards are also given for victory in Chess and Billiards/Snooker. Special Awards are also given to Juniors for winning medals in the World, Asian and Commonwealth Championships. The basic objective of the awards is to provide an incentive to the achievers and an inspiration to the upcoming sportspersons. It is also intended to help the sportspersons of outstanding calibre to be able to maintain themselves with dignity and continue to give their best in further pursuit of the sports of their choice. For the year 1997-98 it is expected that about 200 sports-persons will be given cash awards.

Sports fund for pension to meritorious sportspersons

Government had launched this scheme from the year 1094. Under the scheme, pension is given to sportpersons who win medals in Olympic games, World Cup/ World Championship, Asian Games and Commonwealth Games. While Olympic Games medalists and Gold medalists of World Cup/world Championship are- given pension @ Rs. 2500/- p.m., Silver and Bronze medalists of World Cup/World Championship, Gold Medalists of Asian Games and Gold Medalists of Commonwealth Games are given pension @ Rs.2000/- per month. Pension is given from the age of 30 through lifetime. The scheme is being operated through the Life Insurance Corporation of India (LIC). At present, 202 sportspersons are receiving pension under the scheme.

National welfare fund for sportpersons

The National Welfare Fund for sportspersons and their families was set up in 1982 primarily to assist outstanding sportspersons of yesteryears, who are living in indigent circumstances. This financial support is given generally in the form of monthly pension up to Rs.2,500. Lump-sum grants are also given for medical treatment. The sportspersons suffering from grievous or fatal injury in the course of participation in sports events during training are also helped. At present 72 sportspersons are receiving pension under the scheme.

Promotion of sports and games in schools

The Scheme was introduced in 1986 with a view to raise the standard of sports at the school level and to encourage participation in inter school competitions. This scheme has been recently revised and the revised scheme came into existence from 1.4.93. Under this scheme, grant is given @ Rs.50,000/- per District and Rs.2 lakh per State to the Directorate of Sports for holding District and State level Inter-school tournaments. The State performing the best National level tournaments will be given an award of Rs.1.00 lakh alongwith a rolling trophy. The scheme will be operated directly by the State Government.

Rural sports programme

Rural Sports Programme was launched in 1970-71 with a view to broadbase games and sports and tap the hidden talent in rural areas. The scheme has two subcomponents, viz., organization of sports tournaments right from the block level to the national level and organization of Sports Festival for the North Eastern Region. The scheme is implemented by the Sports Authority of India.

The sports tournaments at the national level for the year 1998-99 were organized by SAI, in two groups, as per details given below:-

Group	*Venue*	*Duration of Tournament*	*Sports Disciplines*	*Number of Participants*
I	Nellore Andhra Pradesh	16.12.98 19.12.98	Volleyball Football Kho-Kho Archery Weightlifting	999
II	Rohtak (Haryana)	28.12.98 31.12.98	Athletics Hockey Kabaddi Wrestling Tug of War	985
			Total : 1984	

National sports festival for women

The scheme started in 1975 aims at promoting sports amongst women. Under the scheme, national level competitions are preceded by holding of lower level competitions (Block, District & State levels for which States/U.Ts are provided financial assistance as per norms. During 1998-99, the Festival was conducted by SAI in 3 groups covering 12 sports disciplines as per details given below:

Group	*Venue*	*Duration of Tournament*	*Sports Disciplines*	*Number of Participants*
I	Cuttack (Orissa)	14.10.98 to 17.10.98	Badminton Swimming Table Tennis, Tennis	283

II	Nizamabad (Andhra Pradesh)	19.11.98 to 22.11.98	Athletics Handball Kabaddi Volleyball	907
III	Kurukshetra (Haryana)	7.1.99 to 10.1.99	Basketball Gymnastics Hockey Kho-Kho	808
			Total	1998

Sports festival for the north eastern region

The Scheme was launched in the year 1986-87 to broadbase games and sports in the North Eastern States and to tap the hidden talent in the area. The States covered under the Scheme are Arunachal Pradesh, Assam, Manipur , Meghalaya, Mizoram, Nagaland, Sikkim and Tripura. The North-East Sports Festival for the year 1997-98 could not be held due to the Lok Sabha elections held in the region. Details of the North-East Sports Festival for the year 1998-99 are given below:-

Year	*Venue*	*Duration of Festival*	*Sports Disciplines*	*No. of Participants*
1997-98	Imphal (Manipur)	224.11.98 to 27.11.98	Volleyball, Basketball, Table Tennis, Hockey, Judo and Athletics	385
1998-99	Guwahati (Asssam)	29.1.99 to 31.1.99	Athletics, Football, Badminton, Table Tennis and Boxing	306

Assisting promising sportspersons and supporting personnel

This scheme has been formulated by merging two schemes viz., Travel grant to Sports Specialists and Scheme of Scholarship for Training of Specialists and Out-Standing sprotpersons in Sports/Adventure abroad.

Under the scheme, assistance is given to promising sportpersons for training and participation in tournaments abroad, for purchase of equipment, for scientific support and for training and participation in tournaments in the country Supporting personnel are assisted for undergoing specialised training in a particular sports discipline and for training, attending seminars, conferences of repute and major international sports events and appearing in qualifying examination. Assistance will also be provided for holding national training camps for sportspersons and supporting personnel inside the country.

Assistance to national sports federations

Financial assistance is given to National Sports Federations for conducting national championships, for organising coaching camps for preparing teams, and for their participation in international tournaments. Limited secretarial support is also given by way of reimbursement of salary of the paid Joint/Assistant Secretaries of the Federations. The requests for assistance are processed according to the guidelines laid down by the Department. The Indian Olympic Association is also assisted under this scheme.

National level Monitoring Committee under the Chairpersonship of Minister of State, and Discipline-wise Monitoring Committees under the Chairmanship of DG, SAI were constituted for monitoring the preparation of national teams for participation in 1998 Asian and Commonwealth Games.. These Committees will function till 2000 Olympics.

XVI commonwealth games, 1998

The XVI Commonwealth Games were held at Kualalumpur from September 11 -21, 1998. India participated only in six disciplines, viz. Shooting; Weightlifting, Badminton, Hockey (Men & women),

Boxing and Cricket. Government cleared a contingent of 111 sports persons and officials for participation.

In these Games India won 7 Gold, 10 Silver and 8 Bronze medals (25) in 4 disciplines out of the 6 disciplines participated. This medal tally is better than that of the last Commonwealth Games. (The details are given in the Annexure - VI.)

XIII Asian games, 1998

XIII Asian Games, 1998 were held at Bangkok, Thailand from 6th to 20th December, 1998. The total contingent of 310 persons participated in 21 disciplines and won 35 medals (7 Gold, 11 Silver and 17 Bronze Medals), (Details are given in Annexure - VII.) The performance of Indian sportpersons was much better in comparison to the last Asian Games, 1994. Performance of Hockey team (Men) deserves special mention as the team has won Gold Medal after a gap of 32 years. In Athletics, Ms. Jyotirmoyee Sikdar has come out as a bright star winning two gold medals. Similarly, in Boxing Shri Dingko Singh and in Billiards Shri Geeth Sethi and Shri Ashok Shandilya also deserve glowing tributes. Such brilliant success was possible because of the support and cooperation extended by all those concerned with sports.

Besides these, 103 proposals of National Sports Federations for foreign exposures/ visits at Government Cost and 76 proposals at No Cost to Government were cleared. (The details of these proposals are given at Annexure - VIII.)

During 1998-99 upto 3.2.99, an expenditure of Rs.725.00 lakh under Plan and Rs.160.00 lakh under Non-Plan has been booked.

Arjuna awards

The Arjuna Award was instituted in 1961 as the highest national recognition of distinguished sportpersons. The awardee is given a bronze statute of Arjuna, a scroll and a cash prize of Rs.50,000.00. The awardee is also provided a ceremonial dress.

Arjuna Awards for the year 1997 were presented by the Hon'ble President of India to 21 outstanding sportpersons at Rashtrapati Bhawan on 29th August, 1998. The total number of sportpersons who have so far been given Arjuna Awards is 492.

Physical education

The Lakshmibai National Institute of Physical Education was established initially as College on 17th August, 1957, the centenary year of the first war of India's Independence. The Institute is located at Gwalior, where Rani Lakshmibai of Jhansi had dedicated her life to the country's glory.

In recognition of the services rendered by the Institute in the field of physical education and sports, it has been upgraded to a 'Deemed to be a University' status in 1995. The Institute is an autonomous organization under the administrative control of the Department and is registered under the Societies Registration Act. 1973. The Institute is fully funded by the Government of India . During1998-99, it was assisted by the following grants-in-aid-

i)	Grant-in-aid (Plan)	–	Rs. 2263.00 lakkh
ii)	Grant-in-aid (N. Plan)	–	Rs. 225.00 lakh
iii)	Income generated by the Institute	–	Rs. 53.00 lakh
	Total		Rs. 541.00 lakh

During the year 1998-99 the Institute offered the following full time courses:

1) Bachelor of Physical Education (BPE) (3 year course)

2) Master of Physical Education (MPE) (2 year course).

3) MPE (Summer Course) (3 year course) for in-service teachers.

4) M.Phil in Physical Education (1 year course)

The Institute also conducted in service training programmes in Physical Education for ex-army Personnel, refresher/orientation course for physical education teachers in universities, colleges and schools. The total class-wise strength of the students in the current session is given as under :-

Sl. No.	*Class*	*Boys*	*Girls*	*Total Students*
1.	BPE - I	77	31	108
2.	BPE - II	64	33	97
3.	BPE - III	71	32	103
4.	MPE -(Prev.)	45	19	64
5.	MPE -(Finl.)	31	09	40
6.	M. Phil	04	01	05
		292	125	417

The Institute attracts students from abroad also. 3 Girls & 13 Boys from Mauritius joined the Institute during the current Academic Session.

Total number of graduates, post graduates, M.Phil and Ph.D. students passed out from the institute till academic year 1998 is as follows:

S1. No.	*Course*	*Total*
i)	Graduates	2816
ii)	Post Graduates	1485
iii)	M.Phil	186
iv)	Ph.D	112

During the academic session 1998-99, 126 male and 51 female candidates were selected for admission to BPE -1, MPE(Previous), M. Phil., MPE (Summer Course) - 1. A total of 30 research projects have also been approved for MPE and M.Phil during the current academic session. The Institute has a staff strength of 216 in total.

The Institute has the following facilities:-

(a) The Library of the Institute has a separate reference section for post-graduate and research scholars with various facilities. The Library has about 30,000 volumes on physical education and allied subjects.

(b) The Institute has following laboratories equipped with indigenous and imported equipment :-

   (i) Human Performance

   (ii) Sports Psychology

   (iii) Bio-Mechanics

   (iv) Measurement and Evaluation

   (v) Kinanthropometry

   (vi) Teaching Methodology

   (vii) Sports Bio-chemistry and Data Analysis.

(c) The Institute has excellent playfields and has facilities for gymnasium, swimming, cricket, squash, football, hockey, basketball, tennis, volleyball, Kho-Kho, Kabaddi, badminton, throw-ball, tennis, and table tennis.

(d) The Institute has a 'Health Education and Sports Medicine Division' with related facilities. It caters to the health needs of the students and staff.

After grant of 'Deemed to be a University' status,

the Institute has come of age and is expected to progress fast. It is hoped that the Institute will become a model for all institutions in the field of physical education in the country.

National sports development fund

A national Sports Development Fund has been created by the Central Government with a view to mobilising resources from Government as well as other non-Government Sources, such as private and corporate sector, Non-Resident Indians etc. for the promotion of sports and games. With a view to making the contribution to the fund attactive, 100% exemption from income tax on all contributions made to the fund has been granted.

10

International Cooperation

Exchange of youth delegations at international level

In order to widen the horizons of our youth, it is necessary that they are exposed to the developments taking place in social, economic cultural and other fields in the rest of the world. Similarly, it is necessary for us to project our cultural values and progress among other countries. The International Exchange of Youth Delegations is conceived as an effective instrument for promoting exchange of ideas and to develop better relations with other countries. Under this programme youth delegations are exchanged with other countries for participation in various youth programmes, meetings, seminars conferences, etc.. It is also proposed to lay increasing emphasis on exchange of delegations in the Asian continent, especially among SAARC countries. The following visits were taken up during 1998-99:-

1. A 5-member Indian delegation visited Moscow from 16th to 23rd April, 1998 under Indo-USSR Youth Protocol.
2. A-3 member Indian delegation visited Colombo (Sri Lanka) to attend the Workshop on Promoting Enterprise and Economic Development from 25th April to 31st May, 1998.
3. Joint Secy. (Youth Affairs) visited Macao to participate in the Regional Consultation of

Youth Organisations from Asia and Pacific region on Youth Voluntary Service from 3rd to 7th April, 1998.

4. A 4-member Indian delegation led by Minister of State (Ms. Uma Bharati) attended the Commonwealth Youth Ministers Meeting (CYMM) and the meeting of Committee of Management and Regional Advisory Board held at Kuala Lumpur (Malaysia) from 25 th to 31st May, 1998.

5. Joint Secy. (Youth Affairs) visited Bangkok (Thailand) from 31st May to 5th June, 1998 to attend the 2nd Asia Pacific Inter-Governmental Meeting on Human Resource Development for Youth.

6. Secretary (Youth Affairs & Sports) visited London from 21st to 27th June, 1998 to attend Joint Body Meetings of the Commonwealth Secretariat Finance Committee, the CFTC Board of Representatives and the Chairpersons of the Commonwealth Youth Programme and Communication Science Council (CSC) of the Commonwealth Secretariat.

7. A 3-member Indian delegation participated in the World Youth Forum of the UN System held in Braga (Portugal) from 2nd to 6th August, 1998.

8. Secretary (Youth Affairs & Sports) and Joint Secy(Youth Affairs) visited Lisbon (Portugal) from 8th to 12th August, 1998 to attend the World Conference of Ministers Responsible for Youth.

9. A 28-member Indian teachers delegation visited Japan from 25.11-98 to 22.12.98 under Japan

South Asia Youth Friendship Programme to study the education system at secondary level schools in Japan.

10. Secretary (Youth Affairs & Sports) visited Barbados 20th-21st November, 1998 to attend Commonwealth Ministerial Review Meeting.

11. A 4-member Indian delegation visited Singapore to attend Regional Training Workshop on Family Values from 28 th November to 2nd December, 1998.

12. A delegation led by Hon'ble Dato' Shahrizat Abdul Jalil, Parliamentary Secretary, Government of Malaysia visited India from 8th to 15 th November, 1998, on the invitation of CYP Asia Centre, Chandigarh.

13. 12 Youth delegates from SAARC countries participated in the National Youth Festival held at Lucknow from 12 th to 16 th January, 1999.

14. A 5-member Indian delegation participated in the Regional Training Workshop on Management Skills for Youth Organisations hold in Colombo, Sri Lanka from 26th January to 6 th February, 1999.

15. Mauritius Minister of Youth and Sports and Permanent Secretary, Government of Mauritius visited India from 27th January to 5th February, 1999 and Sports and Youth Protocols were signed between the Department of Youth Affairs and Sports, Government of India & Ministry of Youth & Sports, Government of India Mauritius.

Commonwealth youth programme

The establishment of a Commonwealth Youth Programme (CYP) was first proposed at the

Commonwealth Heads of Government meeting in 1969. The Programme came into being in 1974 with the overall purpose of promoting the development of young men and women in the Commonwealth. The Programme has the following main objectives:-

i) to encourage and support the active participation of youth in the process of national development.

ii) to give recognition to the contribution made by the youth to the economic,

iii) to promote productive activity in its widest sense with a view to eliminating unemployment and alleviating its ill-effects;

iv) to provide opportunities for increasing international understanding among youth; and

v) to provide and encourage activities in furtherance of the foregoing objectives.

The following activities constitute the core work method of CYP for achieving the above objectives:-

i) Training - including diploma level courses for youth and development workers; short courses and distance learning initiatives;

ii) Support to youth projects - through seed funding and technical assistance;

iii) Publications - covering training materials, policy documents and newsletters and relevant youth work information;

iv) Youth exchange - enabling young people to visit different Asian countries and know their cultures,

v) Study fellowship - assisting youth work officials to study areas of interest in different countries.

The headquarters of CYP is located at the Commonwealth Secretariat, London. Besides, there are four Regional Centres located as under:-

i) Lusaka (Zambia) for the African Region,

ii) Chandigarh (India) for the Asia Region,

iii) Georgetown (Guyana) for the Carribean Region, and

iv) Suva (Fiji) for the South Pacific Region.

The programmes are mainly financed by member countries. India's contribution to CYP programmes during 1998-99 will be 81,596 Pound sterling (a 3% increase over last year's contribution). This will be equivalent to Rs.59.00 lakhs. Besides, as a host country for regional centre for Asia Region, India has provided building and other basic infrastructural facilities for the Asia Centre at Chandigarh.

CYP Asia Centre, Chandigarh launched the CYP Diploma in Youth Development through distant mode. The modules of the course have been developed by CYP and the responsibility of conducting the Diploma Course has been assigned to IGNOU.

Secretary, Department of Youth Affairs & Sports has been elected as chairperson of the Committee of Management of the Commonwealth Youth Programme, which is the highest Committee after the Committee of Youth Ministers of Commonwealth Countries.

Exchange of sports and physical education teams/experts

International cooperation in the field of sports & physical education took a big leap forward, providing the much-needed opportunities of foreign exposure to national teams and coaching/training abroad. Government of India procured the services of international coaches/sportpersons by way of bilateral agreements under

Cultural Exchange Programmes/Sports protocols with the concerned countries. The foreign coaches are paid air-fare, tax free salaries, TA&DA, medical expenses and local transportation, etc. during their contract/ employment in India.

During the year, Government has approved appointment of 15 foreign coaches/ experts in Athletics, Archery, Boxing, Judo, Kayaking, Wrestling, Weightlifting, Sports Medicine, Sports Massage and General Theory & Methods of Training (GTMT) Expert for imparting training to Indian sportpersons.

United Nations volunteers

Created in 1970 and operating under the United Nations Development Programme (UNDP), United Nations Volunteers (UNV) is world's unique multilateral volunteer sending scheme and has become one of United Nations' foremost supplier of middle and upper level specialist professionals at low cost, who work with national and international personnel in over 143 developing countries of Africa, Asia, the Pacific, Central and Latin America, the Carribean, CIS & Baltic countries and the Middle East in a wide variety of technical, economic, professional and social fields offering practical response to their developmental needs.

India has been participating in the UNV Scheme very actively right from its beginning. Presently, 39 Indian nationals are working abroad as UNVs and 114 Men and 48 Women are on the roster of UNDP awaiting assignment. The volunteers are not given any formal pay and allowances. But, they get a monthly living allowance ranging from US $ 560 to 1783 depending upon the marital status of the candidate, nature of the assignment and the local conditions of the host country. They also get modest housing and utilities and local transport, health and life insurance, settling in-grant and resettlement allowance on completion of the assignment. India also contributes to the special Voluntary "Fund of UNDP" and the current level of India's contribution is US$ 15,000 per year.

There is another component of the UNV Scheme known as the UNV-Domestic Development Service (DDS). Under DDS, India sends volunteers selected from various voluntary organisations, Nehru Yuva Kendras etc. to neighbouring countries like Nepal, Sri Lanka, Indonesia, Malaysia, Bangladesh, etc. to work at grassroots level for assisting in the self-help efforts of the' local communities. Presently, 4 Indian DDS volunteers are working abroad. They are provided with nominal work facilities and paid a monthly living allowance of US$ 250 per month.

On 5th December, 1998 being the International Volunteer Day, this Department organised a Workshop on 'Youth & Voluntary Service' in which, youth, the NGOs and other Government organisations working in various fields of voluntary work exchanged views on the importance of voluntary work for the national development.

11

Organisation

Secretariat

The sanctioned strength of the Department is 196. It consists of 17 Group 'A' Officers (comprising 1 Secretary; 2 Joint Secretaries, 2 Directors, 2 Deputy Secretaries, 1 Programme Adviser, 8 Under Secretaries and 1 Principal Private Secretary; 74 Group B Posts (21 gazetted and 53 non-gazetted); 76 Group 'C' posts and 29 Group V posts. Besides this., there are 13 sanctioned posts in the Personal Staff of Minister of State for Youth, Affairs & Sports. These posts comprise 1 Private Secretary, 1 Additional Private Secretary, 1 Assistant Private Secy., 1 First Personal Assistant, 2 Second PAs, 1 Language PA, 1 Lower Division Clerk, 1 Jamadar, 1 Driver & 3 Peons. There are 36 persons belonging to Scheduled Castes (2 in Gr. W, 10 in Group 'B' (4 gazetted and 6 non-gazetted) 13 in Group 'C' and 11 in Group 'D'. There is one person belonging to Scheduled Tribes in Group V.

Budget allocations

The total budget allocation for the Department for 1998-99 is Rs. 200 Crore. It comprises Rs. 160 Crore on the Plan side and Rs.40 Crore on non-Plan.

Progressive use of Hindi in the department of youth affairs and sports

The Department of Youth Affairs & Sports is equipped with sufficient staff for implementation of Official

Language Policy of the Union and the Official Languages Act enacted thereunder. The staff include the Assistant Director (OL), Senior and Junior Hindi Translators and other helping staff. An Official Language Implementation Committee has been set up under the Chairmanship of the Joint Secretary (Hindi) to look into the problems and solve the same in connection with the implementation of Official Languages Act in the Department of Youth Affairs & Sports and Offices under it and the meetings of this Committee are held from time to time. As a result thereof, all notifications, resolutions, general orders, circulars, memoranda etc. are issued bilingually. All name plates, notice-boards, rubber stamps, seals, letter heads are prepared both in Hindi and English Letters received in Hindi are invariably replied to in Hindi. The Performance Budget and Annual Administrative Report of the Department are laid on the tables of the both Houses of the Parliament both in Hindi and English.

The Department has been notified by the Department of Official Language, under Rules 10(4). A number of Sections of the Department have been specified under Rule 8 (4) for use of Hindi. The officers in the Department who do not possess working knowledge of Hindi are nominated for training to the Prabodh, Praveen and Pragya. Similarly, the typists and stenographers of the Department who do not have knowledge of Hindi Typing and Hindi Stenography are also nominated for training in Hindi typing and Hindi stenography. The Department has under its control a total of 3 subordinate offices, which have been notified under Rule 10 (4) (para). On the pattern of last year, a Hindi fortnight was held during the current year. During the fortnight, a variety of competitions were held for officers and employees and all officers and employees including Secretary participated in these competitions and the contestants gaining 1 st, 2nd and 3rd positions were also awarded by the Secretary. Moreover, in order to accelerate the use of Hindi in the Department of YA&S, appeals were issued at the level of Minister of State for Youth Affairs and Sports and directions given at the level of Secretary, thereby requesting all officers and employees of the Department to use more and more Hindi in their routine official work. In addition, Hindi workshops were organised for all the Section Officers, Assistants, UDCs and LDCs from time to time.

Sufficient monitoring is being conducted for implementation of Official Languages Act in the Department and Offices under its control. Besides, a Hindi Salahkar Samiti (Hindi Advisory Committee) is being reconstituted under the Chairmanship of the Union Minister of Human Resource Development to have proper monitoring of the Official Languages Act in the Department. The best possible efforts were made to achieve the targets set in the Annual Programme prepared by the Dept. of Official Language in the Department of Youth Affairs & Sports and under its control.

Library

The Department also has an informal Library where publications of interest to the Department on subjects like sports and games, yoga, physical education, youth programmes etc. are preserved for reference in the Department. At present, the library has 2447 accessioned publications are there. There are also a good number of other publications of importance but not accessioned, like sports and youth magazines, annual reports of various Ministries/Departments, etc.

Grievances redressal

A Public Grievances Redressal Machinery is existing in the Department for attending to the grievances of the members of public in respect of the performance of the

Department proper and its associated organisations. Joint Secretary Incharge of Administration is the Director of Public Grievances. A separate machinery exists for redressal of the grievances of staff members. Whenever any grievance is received in the Department, it is referred to the authority concerned and a careful watch is kept by the redressal machinery on its expeditious disposal/ settlement.

Computerization

National Informatics Centre (NIC) has installed a Windows NT Server and five client machines in the department of Youth Affairs & Sports. NIC continued to provide consultancy software and hardware support to the department. Highlights of computerization the year 1998-99 are given below.

Local Area Network (LAN) has been established by NIC. The cable was laid and server and hubs (intermediate network unit for connecting many computer systems) were installed by NIC. Twenty machines (486 and above) in the Department have been put on the LAN. Users have been trained for surfing Internet, use of e-mail and sharing resources of the computer systems on the LAN.

A website for the department has been created by NIC. This site contains brief introduction, organizational setup, details of various activities and schemes implemented by the Department and scheme-wise outlays. The website giving information about the department is accessible from any computer in the world having Internet facility. The address of the website of the department is http://www.nic.in/yas. The guidelines and application forms of various scheme of this Department will also be available on the website shortly.

Software for monitoring youth schemes of the

Department is being developed. System analysis & designing has been completed. This package scrutinizes the projects, generates reports for the agenda of Grants-in-aid Committee (GIAC) meetings, prepares minutes of the meetings and sanction order and bills.

Public Grievances monitoring system is being used for monitoring grievances received by the Department and their speedy redressal. The status report is sent to Department of Administrative Reforms and Public Grievances every month. Payroll package is also being used for preparing pay-bills, schedules and pay-slips of the employees of the Department. The file tracking system is being implemented which facilities in tracking various files, their status and helps in speedy disposal.

12

Wakf Administration

The Institution of Wakf is a striking feature of the Islamic jurisprudence, which originated from Islam and developed with it into a full-fledged system. The word "Wakf" applies to any property moveable or immovable, dedicated for purposes recognised by the Muslim Law as religious, pious or charitable. Apart from their religious aspect, the Wakfs are also instruments of social/economic upliftment as the benefits from the Wakfs flow to the needy persons for their socio-economic, cultural and educational development. In India there are lakhs of Wakfs, valued at over hundreds of crores of rupees. Considering their number and value, Wakfs if properly administered, can become a strong instrument not only for the preservation of religious and charitable institutions but also for educational and economic development of the country. Wakfs constitute a national asset as a very large number of them support schools, colleges, technical institutions, libraries, reading rooms, charitable dispensaries, musafir-khanas etc. which benefit the general public irrespective of their caste or creed.

The subject relating to Wakfs (Charitable and religious endowments) figures at S. No. 28 of the Concurrent List of the Seventh Schedule of the Constitution. Supervision over the administration of Wakf is, therefore, the responsibility of both the Central and State Governments.

Responsibility of the ministry

The Ministry is responsible for the administration of (i) The Wakf Act, 1995 (ii) The Durgah Khawaja Saheb Act, 1955, (iii) the work relating to the evacuee Wakf properties under the Administration of Evacuee Property Act, 1950. However, the Central Government has been taking up issues of common concern to promote the interests of Wakfs in the country. Some of these are-

(i) Legislation to strengthen the effectiveness of the Wakf Law;

(ii) Ensuring early completion of survey of Wakf properties by the State Governments;

(iii) Measures to protect Wakf properties from encroachment; and

(iv) Steps to augment the financial resources of the Wakf Boards and Wakf institutions etc.

The Wakf Act, 1995

Since the actual working of the Wakf Act, 1954 brought out many deficiencies in' it as also in the set up of Wakf Boards particularly in their powers of superintendence and control over Wakfs, it was extensively amended through the Wakf (Amendment) Act, 1984 on the basis of recommendations of Wakf Inquiry Committee contained in its final report submitted to the Government in 1976, However, the Wakf (Amendment) Act, 1984 could not be enforced as there was strong opposition to many of its provisions. Therefore, after extensive consultations with all concerned, a new Wakf Law namely the Wakf Act, 1995 was enacted, which aims at providing better administration for Wakfs and Wakf properties. This Act has been enforced in the entire country with effect from 01st January, 1996.

Implementation of the Wakf Act 1995 by the state government

The provisions of the Wakf Act, 1995 are required to be

implemented by the State Government/UT Administrations. However, since its enforcement, the Central Government has been requesting the State Governments, on a regular basis, to implement the provisions of the Act-particularly, those regarding constitution of new Wakf Boards, establishment of Wakf Tribunals and appointment of Survey Commissioners. However, so far only SEVEN State Governments viz., Andhra Pradesh, Gujarat, Karnataka, Madhya Pradesh, Meghalaya, Tamil Nadu and West Bengal and two Union territory Administrations namely those of Dadra & Nagar Haveli and Lakshadweep have constituted the Wakf Boards, under the new Act. The process of constitution of Wakf Boards in Uttar Pradesh and Delhi is reportedly at an advanced stage. Governments of Madhya Pradesh, Rajasthan, Tamil Nadu, Uttar Pradesh, NCT of Delhi and UT of Lakshadweep have established Wakf Tribunals under the new Act. The Wakf Tribunals are being constituted in Karnataka shortly.

So far fourteen (14) State Governments namely those of Andhra Pradesh, Goa, Gujarat, Himachal Pradesh, Karnataka, Kerala, Madhya Pradesh, Maharashtra, Meghalaya, Punjab, Tamil Nadu, Tripura, Uttar Pradesh and West Bengal and four Union Territories of Andaman & Nicobar Islands, Dadra & Nagar Haveli, Lakshadweep and Pondicherry have appointed Survey Commissioners in their respective States/UTs. The matter is being followed up with State Governments/UT Administrations on a regular basis.

Central Wakf council

The Central Wakf Council is a statutory body established by the Central Government under section 8A of the Wakf Act, 1954 [now read as subsection (1) of section 9 of the Wakf Act, 1995] for the purpose of advising it on matters relating to working on the Wakf Boards and proper administration of Wakfs in the country. With the enforcement of the new Wakf Law, the Central Wakf Council, constituted under the provisions of the earlier Wakf Act, 1954, stood dissolved. A new Council consisting of twenty Members was reconstituted on 26th June, 1997. The members appointed were from specific categories like Members of both the Houses of Parliament, Chairmen of Wakf Boards, persons representing Muslim organisations having an All India character, former Judges of Supreme Court or High Court, Mutawallis, eminent scholars in Muslim Law etc. The Union Minister incharge of Wakf is the ex-officio Chairperson of the Council.

Development of Urban Wakf properties

To improve the financial position of the Wakfs and Wakf Boards and to enable them to enlarge the area of their welfare activities, the Central Government has been giving, from 1974-75, annual grants-in-aid to the Central Wakf Council for the specific purpose of advancing loan to the Wakf Boards/Wakf Institutions for the development of Urban Wakf Properties. The projects involve construction or reconstruction of commercially viable buildings on Urban Wakf lands. Upto 1997-98 grant-in-aid amounting to Rs. 1586.11 lakhs has been released to the Council. The budgetary provision for the year 1998-99 was Rs. 149 lakhs, and the whole amount has been released to the Council The grant of Rs. 63.68 lakhs was utilised by the Council to finance three of its on going projects one each in Rajasthan, Maharashtra and Kerala.

Development of Rural Wakf properties

The Central Wakf Council in its 40th meeting hold on 20.05.1998 has approved a scheme for the development of Rural Wakf properties on the same pattern as that of development of urban Wakf properties. Under this scheme, the Council will provide loan assistance for taking up economically viable schemes upto Rs. 10.00 lakhs from out of its 'Revolving Fund'. The terms and conditions for the scheme will be the same as are applicable in the case of scheme of development of urban Wakf properties. All State Wakf Boards have been informed about the scheme.

Educational schemes

The Central Wakf Council implements welfare activities in the field of education also. The educational schemes being implemented are awarding scholarships to students of technical first degree courses, scholarships to students of IIT, Polytechnic, Madras education, aid to poor & needy students, 50% matching grant to Technical Institutions for starting fresh trade courses or strengthening the existing trade courses and financial assistance to Voluntary Organisations for Vocational Training courses. The amounts spent by the Council during 1998-99 (upto 10.12.1998) on these activities are as follows:

Sl. No.	*Welfare Activity*	*Expdt. Incurred*	*No of Beneficiaries*
1.	Scholarship to Students of Technical Degree Courses. (continuing)	Rs. 17.04 lakhs	355 students @ Rs. 4800/- - per student
2.	Scholarship to fresh student of Technical degree courses	Rs. 15.122 lakhs	3315 students @ Rs. 4800/ - per student
3.	Ad-hoc grant to poor & needy Technical degree courses	Rs.1.97 lakhs	82 students @ Rs. 4800/- - per student

(Contd. . .)

3.	Ad-hoc grant to poor & needy students	Rs. 1.97 lakhs	82 students @ Rs. 2400/- - per student
4.	50% Matching Grant to Technical Institutes.	Rs. 7.00 lakhs	8 Institutes
5.	Financial assistance to Voluntary Organisations for Vocational Training Courses	Rs. 17.00 lakhs	36 Organisations
6.	Financial assistance for readings rooms/ libraries	Rs. 5.30 lakhs	76 Institutes
	Total	Rs 63.43 lakhs	

Participation by central Wakf council in the social development fair held during May, 1998

The Central Wakf Council participated and exhibited its various welfare programmes in the Social Development Fair conducted by the Indian Trade promotion Organisation at Pragati Maidan, New Delhi during May, 1998. This resulted in general awareness about Council's schemes as later on became evident from increased number of applications received in Council's office from various parts of the country for availing the benefits of the schemes run by the council.

Punjab Wakf board

The Punjab Wakf Board, having jurisdiction in the States of Punjab, Haryana and Himachal Pradesh and the Union Territory of Chandigarh, is the only composite Wakf Board in the country and is under administrative control of the Central Government. The Board was first constituted in October, 1960 under the provisions of the Wakf Act, 1954. It was superseded in November, 1981 and since then it is being administered by the Central Government through an Administrator. The present period of supersession is upto the 30th April, 1999.

There are approximately 36,000 Wakf properties in the region, including those which are under adverse occupation and litigation. The Board collects rent and lease amount on the properties which are under tenancy and that is the only source of Board's income.

The annual income of the Board has steadily risen since 1981. The annual income for the year ending 31st March, 1998 was Rs. 8.75 crores as against Rs. 7.15 crores during 1996-97.

The Punjab Wakf Board is a premier welfare organisation in the region with its Head Office at Ambala Cantt. It is engaged in developmental, educational, welfare and charitable activities in the area.

Education

The Muslim Community in the area is educationally back-ward and therefore the Punjab Wakf Board has made several efforts for advancement of education among the Community. There are as many as 10 schools, 4 Wakf Computer Centres and 9 Wakf Tailoring Centres; being run under the direct management of the Board/ Besides, private organisations of Muslims engaged in educational activities are also assisted by the Board by way of monthly aid to them. The Board is providing monthly financial assistance to 46 such schools and 4 vocational centers under its jurisdiction. During the year (fill 15.12.1998) the Board has spent an amount of Rs. 57.78 lacks approximately on this account.

Welfare

The Board has a scheme for providing monthly aid to various Mosques, Madrasas/Dini Maktabs. Till 15-12-

1998 a sum of Rs. 24.40 lakhs was spent on this account against a budget provision of Rs. 42.60 lakhs.

The Board provides monthly pension to the Muslims widows of the region at the rate of Rs. 100-300/-p.m. This scheme has since been extended to cover senior citizens and orphans as well. The number of such beneficiaries now stands at 1590 and till 15.12.1998 an amount of Rs, 98.91 lakhs has been disbursed.

The Board also provides merit-cum-means scholarships to needy Muslim students. 548 such students were granted scholarship amounting to Rs. 5.12 lakhs during the financial year 1997-98.

Till 15.12.1998 grant-in-aid amounting to Rs. 3.06 lakhs was given for maintenance of shrines, schools, madrasas & graveyards etc.

In addition to this till 15.12.1998 an amount of Rs. 6.53 lakhs was disbursed for special repairs of shrines and Mosques etc.

Charity

The Board provides financial to the destitute and needy poor Muslims for-medical treatment, marriages and on other occasions. The Board has also provided assistance at the time of natural calamities, accidents etc. During the year under report (till 15.12.1998), a sum of Rs. 1.87 lakhs has been spent on charity.

Development

The Board also constructed shopping complexes office blocks etc. to augment its resources. In addition to this, construction of off ice-cum-residential accommodation has also been taken-up at many circles of the board. On this head the Board has a spent an amount of Rs. 5.47 lakhs till 15.12.1998.

V. Urs and festivals

The Board organises celebrations on the occasion of annual Urs at Dargahs of famous Sufi Saints, Prominent among them, are those of Hzt. Booali Shah Qalandar, Hzt. Shamshuddin Turk Panipati and Hzt. Jalakiddin Kabirul Aulia at Panipat, Hzt. Sain Tawakkal Shah and Hzt. Lakkhi Shah at Ambala City, Miranji Bhik at Thaska. (Kurukshetra), Hzt. Imam Nasiruddin at Jalandhar and Haji Rattan at Bathinda. Functions are also held at different places on the occasion of Id-e-Miladun-Nabi, Board's Foundation Day and Iftaar etc. During the year under report a sum of Rs. 1.84 lakhs has been spent on this account (till 15.12.1998).

New development initiatives at a glance

1. Plans for establishment of Composite Colleges in Muslim belts like Malerkotla, Nuh & Chamba.
2. Plans for construction of Maternity Hospital & Computer College at Malerkotla & Chandigarh.
3. Mobile Dispensary to cater the basic health need of Muslim community in Sangrur, Malerkotla, Ludhiana & Jalandhar.
4. Creation of New Wakfs.
5. Purchase of plots for development projects from HUDA, PUDA & HPUDA.

Maulana Azad education foundation

Maulana Azad Education Foundation has been setup as a society with the objective of promoting education amongst the educationally backward sections of the society, minorities in particular and others in general. The Government is giving grants-in-aid to the Foundation under a Plan Scheme for building up a 'Corpus Fund' meaning thereby that while the principal amount would remain intact; interest accrued there on would be utilised by the Foundation for financing its different activities. Upto 1997-98 the total corpus amounted to Rs. 70.01 crores. As this amount was considered inadequate to meet the requirements of the Foundation, the Government is considering to augment the Corpus Fund of the Foundation suitably. A sum of Rs. 30 crores exists in the Budget Grant 1998-99 of the Ministry for this purpose out of which the interest amount of Rs. 3.60 crores has been released to the Foundation. There is a overwhelming response to the educational schemes of the Foundation from all over the country. Upto 30th November, 1998, the Foundation has sanctioned a total grant-in-aid of Rs. 23.56 crores (approx.) to 183 NGOs spread in 19 States/U.Ts. Out of this sanctioned amount a sum of Rs. 15.17 crores (approx.) has already been disbursed/released to 156 NGOs for the purpose of establishment expansion of schools/residential schools/ colleges mainly for girls, construction of laboratory buildings, establishment of computer centres-Vocational training centres for women etc.

During the year, 1998-99, the Foundation has sponsored a batch of 16 girls for "Training Programme in Lace-Making" at Infant Jesus Technical & Educational Institution, Mulagumoodu, Dist. Kanyakumari (Tamil Nadu). During this year the Foundation is likely to launch two new schemes of remedial coaching and pre-examination coaching to be carried out by various NGOs.

Dargah Khawaja Saheb, Ajmer

The Dargah of Khawaja Moinuddin Chisty (R.A.) at Ajmer in Rajasthan is a Wakf of International fame. The Dargah is being administered under a Central Act known as the Dargah Khawaja Saheb Act, 1955. This endowment is managed by a Committee known as the Dargah Committee consisting of not less than 5 and not more than 9 members appointed by the Central Government.

The Committee is required to look after the administration, upkeep and maintenance of Dargah endowment.

The Committee is assisted by an Officer known as Nazim who is also appointed by the Central Government. The Nazim exercises powers of control, supervision and management of Dargah endowment under the directions of Dargah Committee. During the current year i.e. 1998-99 upto 30/11/198 an amount of Rs. 1.12 crore was received by way of donations, contributions and rent from Dargah Guest House. The Dargah Committee sanctioned a budget of Rs. 1.93 Crores towards expenditure on upkeep and maintenance of Dargah Sharif during the year 1998-99.

The 786th Annual Urs of Hazrat Khawaja Moinuddin Chisty (R.A.) was celebrated in a befitting manner wherein lakhs of devotees irrespective of faith, caste and creed flocked together to pay homage to the great saint.

A large number of dignitaries and V.I.Ps. from all over the country and neighbouring countries also visited the Dargah during the period under report.

In order to cater to the needs of ever increasing number of Zaireen (devotees), the Dargah Committee has undertaken construction of a new Guest House at an estimated cost of Rs. 80.00 lakhs. The guest house, likely to be completed by March, 2000, will have 40 rooms with attached bathroom and also three dormitories with attached facilities.

A water treatment plant has also been installed at the cost of Rs. 4.5 lakhs for the benefits of the Zaireens.

The Dargah committee is also running a madrasa named Darul Uloom Moinia Usmania with success. During the year under report there were 100 students including 37 students from outside Ajmer. Four students have completed HIFZ (learning of Holy Quram by heart) and were awarded 'Sanad' (certificate) by the Durgah Committee.

The following welfare schemes are also being, implemented by the Dargah Committee for poor an needy. The expenditure incurred upto 30.11.1998 on these schemes is shown below against each—

1.	Langer (free meal)	:	Rs. 1.32 Lakhs
2.	Stipend to widows	:	Rs. 1.91 Lakhs
3.	Aid to needy persons	:	Rs. 0.58 Lakhs
4.	Free Medical Aid	:	Rs. 0.69 Lakhs
5.	Burial of unclaimed dead bodies	:	Rs. 0.79 Lakhs
6.	Coaching and guidance center	:	Rs. 1.00 Lakh

The Accounts of Dargah Sharif are begin audited I Accountant General (Audit), Rajasthan.

13

Welfare of Persons with Disabilities

Demographic profile

Estimates of the number of persons with disabilities vary, depending on the definitions, the methodology and the extent of use of scientific instruments in identifying and measuring the degree of disability, The National Sample Survey Organisation (NSSO) conducted in 1981 a country-wide survey covering 3 types of disabilities i.e., visual, communication and locomotor disabilities. It identified 12 million persons as having at least one or the other disability-constituting about 1.8% of the estimated total population. In the year 1991, NSSO again conducted a country wide survey covering (i) visual (ii) hearing, (iii) speech and (iv) locomotor disabilities. About 16.15 million people were estimated to have one or the other of the types of disabilities mentioned above, This constitutes 1.9% of the total estimated population of the country. It has been observed that for the country as a whole, prevalence of physical disability was 20 per thousand persons in the rural area and 16 in the urban area, Between the two sexes, the prevalence is marginally more among males than among females.

Persons with mental retardation were excluded from both the surveys. However, a sample survey, conducted by NSSO in 1991, for persons with delayed mental development between 14 age group, estimates that about

3% of the estimated child population have delayed mental development. Certain studies conducted by some institution/NGOs suggest that about 2.5% of the estimated population suffer from mental retardation,

The number of leprosy-affected persons is estimated to be about 4 million, of whom about 1/5th are children. About 15 to 30% cam are with deformities. In 196 districts in the country, the prevalence rate is more than 5 per thousand. About 430 million persons live in these high endemic districts.

Disaility Division for the various schemes for the welfare of Disabled persons has the Budget provision of Rs. 165.35 crores for the year 1998-99.

Implementation of the persons with disabilities (Equal Opportunities, protection of rights and full participation) Act, 1995

The implementation of the provisions of the Act require a multi-sectoral collaborative approach of all concerned Ministeries of the Central Government, the State/UT Governments and other appropriate authorities, While in the area of prevention, early detection and intervention, Ministry of Health & Family Welfare and Department of Women & Child Development have to play a major role, in the area of education of children with disabilities, Department of Education has to integrate these programmes within their schemes/programmes. For the creation of barrier free environment, the Ministries of Urban Area and Employment, Surface Transport, Railways and Civil Aviation have to take various positive steps. In the area of employment and training, Ministry of Labour has an important role. Appropriate Government ensures the implementation of the Persons with Disabilities (Equal Opportunities, Protection of Rights and Full Participation) Act, 1995 by making necessary institutional arrangements and implementing various programmes for the people with disabilities within the limits of their economic capacity and development. In order to effectively implementing the provisions of the Act, the following measures have been taken by the Minis".

(i) The National Handicapped Finance & Development Corporation has been operationalised with effect from 24-10,97 to support enterpreneurial activity by the disabled.

(ii) Notification of Central Co-ordination Committee as per Section 3 of the Act, The Committee has undertaken two meetings so far.

(iii) Central Executive committe has been notified. The committee took two meetings so far.

(iv) The Chief commissioner for Persons with Disabilities has been appointed and he has assumed the office w.e.f. 1.9.98.

(v) Five Core Groups of experts and relevant Ministeries have been set up to make recommendations and formulate schemes to give effect to various provisions of the Act.

(vi) Rules under section 73(1) and (2) have been notified.

(vii) National Trust for Welfare of Parsons with Autism, Cerebral Palsy, Mental Retardation and Multiple Disability is proposed,to be set up.

(viii) The Rehabilitation Council of India which is a statutory body for standardisation and training of rehabilitation professional recognition of training institutions and registration of professionals, has recently taken up a comprehensive plan for manpower in disability rehabilitation throughout the country. Sufficient Funds have been allocated to Rehabilitation Council of India (RCI) for this purpose.

(ix) Many State Governments have constituted State Coordination Committee and State Executive Committee to redress the grievances of the disabled persons.

(x) A Central Sponsored Scheme called National Programme for Rehabilitation of Persons with Disabilities has also been proposed for establishing necessary infrastructure to realise fully the objectives of the Act.

(xi) A conference of State Secretaries, in-charge of persons with disabilities was held on 12.2.97 at New Delhi to discuss the implementation of the Act. A Workshop of State Education Secretaries and State Labour Secretaries was also held at New Delhi to sensitise the State Officials.

(xii) An inter-ministerial Group has been constituted to monitor the progress made by the Central Ministries who have specific obligations under the Act.

(xiii) A two-day Conference on Social Economic Perspective for 'Development of the North Eastern States' was held in November, 1998 under the Chairmanship of MOS(SJ&E). It reviewed the effective implementation of the PWD Act and other schemes of the Disability Division in the North-Eastern States. It was attended by the Ministers for Welfare of these States and other important State Government functionaries.

National Institutes

In Consonance with the policy of providing a complete package of welfare services to the physically and mentally disabled individuals and groups and in order to effectively deal with the multi dimensional problems of the disabled population, the following national institutes have been set up in each major area of disability:-

(i) National Institute for the Visually Handicapped Dehradun.

(ii) National Institute for the Orthopedically, Handicapped, Calcutta.

(iii) Ali Yavar Jung National Institute for th~ Hearing Handicapped, Mumbai.

(iv) National Institute for the Mental Handicapped, Secunderabad.

These Institutes are fore-runners as well as trend setters in their respective areas of specialisation. They have been staffed with talented professionals and equipped with modern and scientific equipment: They offer a variety of long-term training programme ranging from three year Degree courses Physiotherapy, Occupational Therapy, Mental retardation, Education of the deaf, Communication Disorders as well as degree and diploma courses for shorter periods in the above disciplines as well as prosthetic and orthotic engineering and audiology speech therapy and teachers training for the blind. These different courses are conducted either at the Institute's headquarters or in their regional centres located in different parts of the country. The role the Institutes is significant, firstly, because of the dearth of trained personnel and facilities for such training in the country to cater to the wide spectrum of needs of the disabled and secondly because the need for filling the gap which was essential owing to the commitment of the Government to provide comprehensive services to the disabled in I country. The clinical and rehabilitation units of the Institutes serve as an in-house laboratory for I trainers as well as the trainees and serve as sounding board for some of the research projects taken up by them, apart from providing model clinical and para medical services to the patients.

Besides the regular academic courses, institutes conduct a large number of short-term training courses, seminars, orientation courses camps their efforts have provided a forum creating awareness among the community at large for bringing the disabled population closet to organisations working for their welfare for exchange of information, knowledge and experience amongst the academicians, professionals, doctors, village/community level workers and all those associated with various aspects of disability.

Besides, two apex level institutions, namely, Institute for the Physically Handicapped, New Delhi and National Institute of Rehabilitation Training and Research, Cuttack, are also providing training and rehabilitation services and undertaking similar activities as the National Institutes.

Setting up of a national institute for the multiple disabilities

It is proposed to set up a National Institute for Multiple Disabilities for providing rehabilitation services to people with multiple disabilities under one roof. The Institute will provide services like early detection and intervention, Medical rehabilitation educational, rehabilitation, psycho-social rehabilitation etc. It will also undertake manpower development and vocational training programmes. It will conduct a number of short-term and long-term training courses including orientation courses and develop material for creating awareness among the community at large.

The Government of Tamil Nadu has donated 15.8 acres of land at Village Muttukadu near Chennai to the Ministry of Social Justice & Empowerment, for this purpose.

Artificial limbs manufacturing corporation of India, Kanpur

The Artificial Limbs Manufacturing Corporation of India

(ALIMCO) was registered under Section 25 of the Companies Act. 1956 on 25th November, 1972 as a Government company, not for profit. The objectives of ALIMCO include (a) to establish facilities for manufacture of artificial limbs, accessories and constituents thereof, (b) To promote, encourage and develop the availability, supply and distribution, at reasonable cost of artificial limbs, accessories and constituents thereof to needy persons including disabled personnel, hospitals and other welfare institutions.

ALIMCO produces quality Aids and Appliances required for orthopaedically and visually handicapped persons. The products are ISI marked/conforming to standards approved by Bureau of Indian Standards. The product range includes Orthotic (Calipers) and Prosthetic (Artificial Limbs) appliances for both Upper and Lower Extremities, Spinal Braces, Cervical Collars, Traction kits, Rehabilitation Aids like Wheel Chairs, Crutches, Three-wheelers and Special Tools and Equipments required for fitment of Prosthetic; and Orthotic Assemblies by Limb Fitting Centres. ALIMCO will commence manufacture of quality hearing aids in collaboration with M/s Semi-

Conductors Ltd., Chandigarh and Ali Yavar Jung National Institute for the Hearing Handicapped, Mumbai, shortly, ALIMCO is exporting its products to Afghanistan, Bangla Desh, Nepal, UAE, Jordan, Iran, Angola, Cambodia and Uzbekistan.

The Corporation is in the process of manufacturing 1000 sets of below knee floor reaction orthosis kits of composite plastics. This is being done on colloboration with M/s C.P.D.C., Hyderabad.

In its endeavour to meet the growing needs of the physically handicapped population of the country, ALIMCO proposed to augment its manufacturing capacity of wheel chairs & tricycles by setting up Production

Centres (APCs) in Eastern, Southern, Western & Northern regions. Capacity of wheel chair & Tricyles at each of the APC has been envisaged on:-

		Nos. per Annum	
		Phase-I	*Phase-II*
(a)	Wheel Chairs TD2 (51)	1200	3600
(b)	Tricycles TD2 (98)	2400	6000

ALIMCO has Regional Marketing Centres at Calcutta, Mumbai, Chennai, Bhubaneshwar and Delhi. Marketing of products is done through these Regional Marketing Centres with the help of extensive dealer network and direct sales to various National Institutes and voluntary organisations. ALIMCO is also an approved agency for implementing ADIP scheme through which Aids and Appliances are distributed to individual beneficiaries by conducting camps at various places with the assistance of the local administration and voluntary agencies. ALIMCO has provided aid and appliances. 1382 disabled persons under ADIP scheme of Government of India in 97-98.

ALIMCO had participated in the "Ability India" exhibition held in New Delhi between 14th and 20th September, 1998 and "2nd Pride of India Exhibition held at Hanoi (Vietnam) from October 23-26, 1998.

During 1997-98, against a budget provision of 3.00 crores, grant-in-aid of Rs. 2.85 crores was provided to ALIMCO. During 1998-99, against a budget provision Rs. 3.00 crores, grant-in-aid of Rs. 2.45 crores was provided to ALIMCO under plan, upto 31.12.98.

National handicapped finance and development corporation (NHFDC)

1. The National Handicapped Finance and Development Corporation (NHFDC) was

incorporated on 24th January, 1997 under Section 25 of the Companies Act, 1956 as a Government Company not for profit. The registered office of the NHFDC is at Faridabad. NHFDC has an authorised share capital of Rs. 400 crores, divided into 40 lakhs equity shares of Rs. 1000/- each and paid up capital of Rs. 200 crores. The entire equity is held by Government of India. The NHFDC is functioning as an apex Financial institution for routing funds through the channelising agencies authorised by the State Government/UT administrations. The outlay for the current financial year for the NHFDC is Rs. 28 crores.

2. The objectives of the ' NHFDC are to promote economic developmental activities for the benefit of handicapped persons. The Corporation will strive to promote self-employment and other ventures for persons/or groups of persons by way of loans and advances, subject to such income/ economic criteria as may be prescribed by the Government, from time to time. It will also extend loans for persuing general/professional technical education, besides assisting in the upgradation of technical enterpreneural skills.

(i) Self employment in small business, e.g. service/ trading sector

(ii) Assistance to disabled enterpreneurs

(iii) Assistance to disabled for higher studies or professional training

(iv) Assistance to agricultural activities

(v) Scheme to promote manufacturing/production of assistive devices for disabaled persons.

(vi) Assistance for skills and entrepreneurial development programmes.

(vii) Schemes to promote self-employment amongst persons with mental retardation, cerebral palsy and autism.

The corporation would provide loans to persons having disability of 40% or above and whose annual Income does not exceed Rs. 60,000/- per annum in urban areas and Rs. 55,000/- per annum in rural areas. Application for loans will be received and processed by the State Channelising Agency, nominated by respective State Government. They, in turn, will forward such applications with their recommendations to the NHFDC for approval and release of loan. Guidelines for funding of projects under various schemes has been sent by this Ministry to all State Governments/UT Administrations, Channelising Agencies, apex NGOs in the disability sector, National Institutes, DRCs and other concerned institutions and organisations.

(a)	1996-97	Rs. 1.00 crore
(b)	1997-98	Rs. 13.30 crores
(c)	1998-99	Rs. 28.00 crores

Project sanctioned by NHFDC:-(as on 31-12-98)

(i) Andhra Pradesh
Total No. 86
Total Amount: Rs. 67-08 Lakhs

(ii) Orissa
Total No. 182
Total Amount: Rs. 64.40 Lakhs

(iii) Assistance
Development

Rhabilitation council of India (RCI)

The Rehabilitation Council of India is a national level statutory body set up by the Govt. of India tinder the

Rehabilitation Council of India Act, 1992 to enforce uniform standards in the training of Professionals/ Personnel in the field of rehabilitation of the disabled, maintenance of the Central Rehabilitation Register and other connected matters. The Council was re-constituted in June, 1998.

The following three major programmes have been approved for implementation by the Council:

National programme of bridge course

This is to give one time opportunity to all special educators/rehabilitation workers serving people with disabilities to become eligible to register themselves with the council as rehabilitation personnel by taking up just one month duration bridge course.

National programme for training of Medical Officers

This aims at giving 3 days orientation training to over 25,000 medical officers working in the PHCs to orient them towards disability and rehabilitation issues and enable them to make appropriate referrals.

Assistance to organisation for manpower

In order to promote training of teachers, vocational instructors, multi-rehabilitation workers and other professionals, grants are given to the training centres institutions/organisations for conducting Diploma/ Degree courses recognised by the Council, under the above programme.

The RCI Act covers the following categories of Rehabilitation Professionals/Personnel:-

i) Audiologists and Speech therapists
ii) Clinical Psychologists
iii) Hearing Aids and Earmould Technicians
iv) Rehabilitation Engineers and Technicians

v) Special Teachers for education and training the disabled

vi) Vocational Counsellors, Employment Officers and Placement Officers dealing with disabilities.

vii) Multipurpose Rehabilitation Therapists, Technicians

viii) Speech Pathologists

ix) Rehabilitation Psychologists

x) Rehabilitation Social Workers

xi) Rehabilitation Practitioners in Mental Retardation

xii) Orientation and Mobility Specialists

xiii) Community based Rehabilitation Professionals

xiv) Rehabilitation Counsellors/Administrators

xv) Prosthetists and Orthotists

xvi) Rehabilitation Workshop Managers

xvii) Physiotherapists

xviii) Occupational Therapists

xix) Ophthalmic Technicians

The Council has registered 1472 professionals/ personnel so far in the Central Rehabilitation Register and issued certificates to them. The Council has inspected/ recognized 35 institutions during the year to conduct various training programmes. The total number of institutions has increased to 114.

District rehabilitation centre schemes

The District Rehabilitation Centre Scheme (DRC) was initiated by the Ministry of welfare, Government of India, during 1985, to provide comprehensive rehabilitation services to the rural disabled right at their door step in 11 districts of the country. These Centres provide the following services:-

(i) Prevention & early detection;

(ii) Medical intervention & surgical correction;

(iii) Fitment of artificial aids and appliances;

(iv) Therapeutical services such as Physiotherapy, Occupational therapy and Speech therapy;

(v) Provision of training for acquisition of skills through vocational training;

(vi) Job placement in local industries;

Four Regional Rehabilitation Training Centres (RRTCs) have also been set up at Chennai, Mumbai, Cuttack and Lucknow for training and manpower development in the field of rehabilitation, particularly for the DRCs.

Setting up a National trust for the welfare of persons with autism, cerebral palsy, mental retardation and multiple disability

National Trust for the Welfare of Persons with Autism, Cerebral Palsy, Mental Retardation and Multiple Disability is proposed to be set up. An amount of Rs. 1.25 crores has been earmarked for this purpose.

Earlier, the Government had introduced a National Trust for the Welfare of Persons with Mental Retardation and Cerebral Palsy Bill, 1995 in Lok Sabha on 6.2.1995 which could not be taken up for discussion. The Bill has since been modified after extensive consultations with professionals, parent bodies and voluntary organisations in the field of mental retardation and cerebral palsy.

The Trust will provide total care to persons with mental retardation with autism, cerebral palsy and multiple disability and also manage the properties bequeathed to the Turst.

The objectives of the Turst,

(i) To enable and empower persons with disability to live as independently and as fully as possible, within their own families.

(ii) To strengthen facilities to support persons with disability within their own families.

(iii) To extend support to orgnisations of persons with disability or parents and voluntary organisations for need based services during periods of family crisis.

(iv) To address to the concerns of persons with diability, who do not have family support.

(v) To promote measures for the care and protection of persons with disability after the death of their parents or guardians.

(vi) To facilities the realisation of equal opportunities protection of rights and full participation of persons with disabilities.

The Cabinet has approved the setting up of the National Turst for the Welfare of Persons with Autism, Cerebral Palsy, Mental Retardation and Multiple Disability. The Bill is likely to be introduced in the Budget Session in 1999.

Indian spinal injury centre, New Delhi

The Indian Spinal Injury Centre (ISIC) has been set up in collaboration with the Italian Government, to provide comprehensive treatment, rehabilitation services and vocational training and guidance to patients with spinal injury. It is the first centre of its kind in Asia. The Centre would also conduct research in multi-dimensional aspects of rehabilitation of such patients. The machinery and technical expertise were made available to the Centre under Indo-Italian Cooperation from Italy. The Ministry of Social Justice and Empowerment has released one time grant of Rs. 2.50 crores to the ISIC in two instalments during 1989-90 and 1990-91. OPD and diagnostic services are already functional. Further support to ISIC to the extent of Rs. 5.8 crores has been approved for capital expenditure and Rs. 1.5 crores of this has been released. An amount of Rs. 1.67 crores with an escalation of 10% per annurn has also been approved for recurring expenditure from 1997-98 onwards in order to sponsor 30 free beds to the poor patients. During 1998-99, a provision of Rs. 3.00 crores (plan) has been made out of which an amount of Rs. 1.54 crores has been reteased upto 31.12.98 and a plan out lay of Rs. 7.00 crores has been proposed for the year 1999-2000.

Assistance to disabled persons for purchase/fitting of aids and appliances

Under the scheme of Assistance to Disabled Persons for Purchase/Fitting of Aids/appliances, assistance is provided to needy physically disabled persons in procuring durable, sophisticated and scientifically manufactured modern standard aids and appliances to facilitate their physical, social and psychological rehabilitation and integration in the mainstream. The scope of the scheme has been enlarged to include 'corrective surgery, use of mass media for information dissemination, etc., under its ambit.

Eligibility criteria

Indian citizens, irrespective of age and sex, possessing a certificate from a Registered Medical Practitioner can avail benefits under the scheme. Aids/appliances costing from Rs. 50/- to Rs. 6,000/- are provided free of cost if the monthly income of the beneficiary is upto Rs. 5,000/- and at 50% of the cost, if the monthly income is between Rs. 5,001/- and Rs. 8,000/-.

The scheme is implemented by registered Societies/Trusts/Companies and any other Institutions recognised by the Ministry of Social Justice and Empowerment for the purpose. The DRDAs/RCSs, headed by the Collector/District Magistrates are also eligible to implement the scheme. Nehru Yuvak Kendra Sangathans have also been included in the list of agencies/institutions implementing the scheme.

Quuantum of assistance

Aids/appliances which do not cost less than Rs. 50/- and not more than Rs. 6,0004 are covered under the Scheme. These limits will apply to individual items of aid and where more than one aid is required, giving of the same will be permissible and the limits will be applied separately. There is no ceiling on amount of grant to be provided under the scheme. Branches of implementing agencies can be considered for separate grants on fulfilling procedural requirements.

Progress of Implementing the scheme

During 1995-96, against a budget provision of Rs. 13.00 crores, grant-in-aid of Rs. 10.60 crores was provided to 77 implementing agencies. During 199697, the budget provision was Rs. 12.85 crores but grant-in-aid of Rs. 6.86 crores was given to 141 implementing agencies. The lower expenditure was due to the limit fixed on the quantum of grant-in-aid of Rs. 5 to 10 lakhs to an agency, even though the number of agencies assisted in 1996-97 increased appreciably. There was a budget provision of Rs. 8.00 crores (RE) for 1997-98 against which a total expenditure of Rs. 8.94 crores was sanctioned to 124 agencies. During 1998-99 Rs. 25.00 crores (plan) has been allocated, against, which an amount of Rs. 8.35 crores has been released to 94 agencies upto Dec. '98. Plan outlay of Rs. 26.00 crores has been proposed for the year 1999-2000.

National awards for the welfare of people with disabilities

Till 1995, World Day of the Disabled was observed on the 3rd Sunday of March every year. On this day, President of India gives National Awards to the achievers in the following categories-

(i) Best Employer of the People With Disabilities;

(ii) Best Disabled Employee and Self-Employed;

(iii) Best Individual working for the welfare of people with Disabilities:

(iv) Best Institution working for the welfare of people with Disabilities;

(v) Placement Officer;

(vi) Best Institution working for the welfare of People with Disabilities.

From this year, (1998) two more categories of awards have been introduced which are as under:

(a) Outstanding Creative Individual with Disabilities

(b) Outstanding work in the creation of barrier-free environment for people with Disabilities.

In consonance with the Resolution of UN General Assembly, it was decided that 3rd December of every year would be observed as the International Day of Disabled Persons. Accordingly, in 1998, International Day of Disabled Persons was observed on 3rd December in Vigyan Bhavan, Prime Minister of India gave away 49 Awards under the various categories.

Witnessing of republic day parade by disabled children

Disabled children from various pans of Me country are invited to witness Republic Day Parade. Boarding, lodging and travel expenes of the disabled children and their escorts is borne by the Ministry of Social Justice & Empowerment. In 1998, 64 disabled children witnessed the parade from PM's enclosure.

Participation in republic day parade by mentally challenged children

As a new initiative, a group of mentally challenged children trained by CIMR, Thiruvananthapuram, participated in the Republic Day Parade giving the message that given the opportunity they are at pat with the other children. The group was also awarded the second prize by the Ministry of Defence.

National fund for people with disabilities

The National fund for People with Disabilities was created under the Charitable Endowment Act 1890 in the name of National Handicapped Welfare Fund to fulfil the following objectives:-

(i) to promote voluntary sector for creating services for the persons with disability, including prevention, early detection of disabilities, education, training, physical and economic rehabilitation of disabled persons.

(ii) to undertake activities that are incidental and conducive to the above objectives.

The rules/regulations of the Fund were amended vide Gazette Notification (Extraordinary) dated 27.10.1997.

The fund is managed by a Board of Management with Secretary (SJ&E) as Chairperson. The meeting of the Board are held at regular intervals to review the utilization & management of funds and the last meeting was held on 30.6.1998. Financial assistance has been sanctioned to 14 NGOs, 1 DRC, Bhiwani and 1 National Institute, NIVH, Dehradun (UP) for taking up projects under the scheme funded through the Fund.

Financial assistance for the welfare of persons with disabilities

Assistance to voluntary organisation for the disabled

The Scheme was started with a view to provide assistance to voluntary organisations working in the hold of handicapped welfare. It is a comprehensive scheme to cover different areas of rehabilitation physical, psychological, social and economic. Financial support is given upto a maximum limit of 90% of the total project cost, with built-in ceiling for certain items. Financial assistance is also given for projects such as vocational training centres, special schools, counselling centres, hostels, training centres for the personnel and placement services etc.

Year-wise allocation, expenditure, number of NGOs assisted and number of beneficiaries are as under:-

Year	*Allocation (Rs. in crores)*	*Expenditure (Rs. in crores)*	*No. of NGOs*	*No. of Bene-ficiaries*
(1)	*(2)*	*(3)*	*(4)*	*(5)*
1992-93	4.00	77.90	302	42811
1993-94	6.00	8.55	240	60161
1994-95	7.00	14.36	409	141615
1995-96	16.70	16.70	350	118268
1996-97	16.70	16.70	357	118824
1997-98	18.00	17.86	334	119620
1998-99	26.70	14.30 Upto 31.12.98		

Assistance to voluntary organisations for rehabilitation of leprosy cured persons

India has a large population of leprosy affected persons, the estimated figure being 4.50 lakhs. The scheme provides financial assistance to NGOs in phased manner for the rehabilitation of leprosy-cured persons both in rural and urban areas. Assistance is given upto 90% of the project cost. Programmes like awareness generation, early intervention, education and vocational training, economic rehabilitation, social integration, etc. are undertaken under the scheme.

Assistance to organisations for manpower development in the field of mental retardation and cerebral paisy

Under the scheme, assistance is given to NGOs, even to the extent of 100% in some cases, for running courses for teachers in the areas of cerebral palsy and mental retardation. Both recurring and non-recurring items are considered for sanction.

Employment of the disabled

The basic objective of the scheme is to help the disabled persons in getting gainful employment either through Special Cells in normal Employment Exchanges or Special Employment Exchanges for Physically Handicapped located throughout the country. At present there are 39 Special Cells and 51 Special Employment Exchanges. The Scheme is implemented through the State Government/UT Administration. The financial assistance is 100 per cent in case of Special Cells and 80 per cent in the case of Special Employment Exchanges Lists of Special Cells and the Special Employment Exchanges for Physically Handicapped in States

The Total number of disabled persons in the live register of these Employment Exchanges was 3,23,220 in 1992 , 3,37,602 in 1993, 3,40,304 in 1994 and 3,53,743 in 1995. The placements in the same period have been 4306, 4451, 4485 and 3706, respectively

Establishment and development of special schools

The Scheme envisages assistance to the NGOs upto the extent of 90% for establishment and upgradation of special schools in the four major disabled areas-orthopaedic, speech & hearing, visual and mentally retarded. Priority under the scheme is given for setting up of schools in districts where there is no special school at present. There are about 240 districts in the country which are still uncovered. Both recurring and non-recurring expenditure are supported by the Ministry.

Yearwise allocation, expenditure, no. of NGOs assisted and number of beneficiaries are given below:

Year	Allocation (Rs. in crores)	Expenditure (Rs. in crores)	No of NGOs	No. of Beneficiaries
(1)	(2)	(3)	(4)	(5)
1993-94	1.50	0.10	7	295
1994-95	1.50	0.32	42	2731
1995-96	0.75	0.75	28	1675
1996-97	0.38	0.78	22	1427
1997-98	1.25	1.33	42	2216
1998-99 upto 31.12.98	10.00	1.84	–	

Technology development project in mission mode

For providing suitable and cost-effective aids and appliances and improving the mobility and enhancement of employment opportunities for the disabled, the scheme of Science and Technology Project in Mission Mode was launched in 1988. Under this project interdisciplinary S&T efforts are mobilised for generation of new technologies and guiding these to large scale use to meet social needs. The entire project cost is met by Government.

The objectives of the project are to coordinate, fund and direct application of technology for development and utilisation of -(a) suitable and cost effective aids and appliances, and (b) emphasis on education and skill development, leading to enhancement of opportunities for employment, easier living and integration in society. This was for the first time that Government of India launched a coordinated programme for developing aids and appliances for persons with disability. Financial assistance is provided on a 100% basis.

Relief assistance under bilateral agreements

Ministry of Social Justice & Empowerment operates bilateral agreements entered into by the Government of India with the Federal Republic of Germany, Sweden, Switzerland, United Kingdom and United State of America. These arrangements envisage duty free entry into India of donated supplies of relief and rehabilitation of the poor without discrimination of caste, creed or race. Under these agreements, commodities' like food grain, milk powder, cheese, processed food stuff, multi purpose stuff, medicines, multi vitamin tablets, hospital equipments, ambulance, mobile dispensaries, agricultural instruments are received by approved Indian organisations from approved donor organisations - located in the above mentioned 5 countries.

National project to integrate mentally retarded in family and community

A National Pilot Project to integrate mentally retarded in Family and Community was launched in March, 1998, in 6 States namely Kerala, Karnataka, Tamil Nadu, Andhra Pradesh, Delhi and Madhya Pradesh, covering about 7,500 beneficiaries, The Pilot project was implemented by CIMR. Thiruvantanthapuram.

The objectives of the Project, are:

(1) Sensitise the families and empower them to integrate the mentally retarded child in the family and community.

(2) Make early intervention in the lives of 7500 hitherto unreached mentally retarded, particularly from the economically weaker sections and provide them early devlopmental inputs.

(3) Introduce low cost, easy to follow teaching aids and training method relevant to rural and urban setting

as a model for inclusion of all the mentally retarded in the family and community.

(4) Prepare the mentally retarded to receive further developmental and vocational education.

(5) Training of a large number of para-professionals within a short period to extend services in this field.

(6) Create awareness in society to focus on mentally retarded, their problems and rights

Ability India Fair-98

An international exhibition of Assitive Devices for people with Disabilities was held from 14th - to 20 September, 1998 at Pragati Maidan, New Delhi. It was Organised by the Ministry of Social Justice & Empowerment, Government of India. It was the first Exhibition of its kind, which was held to display aids & appliances for the Disabled Persons. The basic objective of the exhibition was to disseminate information on aids and appliances available in India and in other countries. The Exhibition was inaugurated on 14.9.98 by the Hon'ble Minister of State for Social Justice & Empowerment, Smt. Maneka Gandhi, in the presence of Chief guest (Bharat Ratna), Dr. A.P.J. Abdul Kalam, Secretary (SJ&E), Addl. Secretary (SJ&E), Joint Secretary (DD) and Shri Lal Advani.

In the Exhibition, about 100 manufacturers from all over the country and 4 foreign countries, namely, USA, Sweden, Australia and Taiwan participated. The exhibitors displayed latest aids & appliances available & being developed. The 6 National Institutes and a Combined group of S&T Mission Mode also participated. A large number of visitors, including businessmen and people with disabilities visited the exhibition. A keen interest was shown by the visitors in the assistive devices being displayed.

14

Social Defence Programmes

Programmes for plder persons

1999 is being observed as the International Year of the Older Persons. Population Ageing which was perceived until recently to be a concern of the industrialised countries only has become an active issue of the developing countries including India. The population of Older Persons (60+) in India ranks the Fourth highest amongst the countries in the world and by the end of the present century, it will be second only to China. Today India is home to one out of every ten senior citizens of the world. The older population which was 56.7 million in 1991 is expected to grow to over over 76 million by the year 2001 and 137 million by 2021. The proportion of the population aged 60 years and above was 5.1 per cent of the total population in 1901, this rose to 5.4 per cent in 1951, 6.4 per cent in 1981 and is projected to be 7.7 per cent by the year 2001. The decadal per cent growth in the elderly population for the period 1991-2001 would be 37.2 per cent; more than double the rate of increase in the general population. The old age dependency ratio (number of old persons 60 + years) to the working age group 15-59 years) has increased from 9.8 per cent in 1951 to 11.92 per cent in 1981 and is projected to be 12.6 per cent by the year 2001. The index of Ageing indicates that while in 1971 there were nearly 14.2 older persons for every 100 children, this figure will rise to 24.7 per hundred children by 2001. In sum as per United Nations classification, the Indian society will progress from a "mature society" (i.e. elderly population between 4.7 per cent of the total population) to an "Ageing Society" (i.e. elderly population more than 7.0 per cent) by the turn of the century. By then the world is projected to inhabit 612 million older persons, which would be 9.8 per cent of the world's population. In other words, one out of every seven elderly person would be from India by the year 2001.

The Changing demographic profile of the country has been accompanied by a new societal order. The traditional norms and values of the Indian Society laid stress on showing respects providing care for the aged. Consequently, the aged members of the family were normally taken care of in the family itself. In recent times the rapid socio-economic transformation has affected every aspect of traditional Indian society. Industrialization with resultant urbanisation and migration of population have affected Institutions like the Age old joint family. Technological advancement, impact of mass media and higher degree of mobility have influenced long established life styles, conventional value systems and customary place of women in the society. Thus the society is witnessing a gradual but definite withering of the joint family system as result of which section of the family, primarily the elders, are exposed to emotional neglect and to lack of physical support.

As result of demographic changes and the changing family context, it can no longer be assumed that the older persons live comfortably at home receiving care from members. Given the trend of Population Ageing in India, the older persons face a number of problems ranging from absence of ensured and sufficient income to support themselves and their dependents, to ill-health to absence of social security, to loss of a social role and recognition, to non-availability of opportunities for creative use of free time. The trend clearly reveals that Ageing will become a major social challenge in the future and vast resources will be required towards the support, care and treatment of the older persons. There is an emerging need to pay greater attention to Ageing issues and to promote holistic policies and programmes for dealing with a future Ageing society.

The Ministry of Social Justice & Empowerment is the nodal Department of the Govt. of India for matters relating to older persons. The Ministry is implementing a Central Scheme of Assistance for Programmes relating to the Aged since November, 1992. Under the Scheme, financial assistance is provided to voluntary organisations for establishing and maintaining Old Age Homes, Day Care Centres, Mobile Medicare Units and for supporting and strengthening Non-Institutional services for the Aged. During 1996-97 a new Scheme of Assistance to Panchayati Raj Institutions/Voluntary Organisation for Construction of Old Age Homes was initiated. The Scheme aims at providing at least One Old Age Home per District. The assistance under the Scheme is one time construction grant.

National policy for older persons

In keeping with the growing importance of the subject a National Policy for Older Persons was announced by the Government in January, 1999. The principle areas of intervention and action strategies suggested in the policy' for the sector include the following:

(1) Financial Security for Older Persons working in the formal sector as well as those working in the informal sector;

(2) Health Care & Nutrition to enable Older Persons to cope up with health and associated problems

commonly associated with old age with particular emphasis upon preventive strategies;

(3) Shelter/housing keeping in view the life style of older persons;

(4) Emphasis upon education, training and information needs of older persons;

(5) Priority attention to especially vulnerable group such as the destitutes, widows and the disabled older persons;

(6) Establishment of a welfare fund for Older Persons:

(7) Special attention to protection of life and property of Older Persons;

(8) Provision of appropriate concessions, rebates and discounts to Older Persons;

(9) Full participation of the Non-Governmental Organisation in the sector;

(10) Formation of self-help groups of older persons;

(11) Productive Ageing;

(12) Strengthening of the family and reinforcing inter-generational relationships between children and Older Persons;

(13) Promotion of research and advocacy in the field;

(14) Development of trained manpower in the sector particularly in medical colleges and schools of social work;

(15) Creative use of media to promote concepts such as life long preparation for old age, productive ageing and building a society for all ages;

(16) Establishment of a separate bureau for Older Persons in the Ministry;

(17) Preparation of sectoral Annual and Five Year Plans on the subject;

(18) A detailed review to be carried out of the implementation of the National Policy every three years;

(19) Establishment of a National Council for Older Persons;

(20) Establishment of a National Association of Older Persons;

(21) Use of Social Justice Committee of the Village Panchayats for giving effect to the policy;

(22) Use of experts of Public Administration to coordinate and monitor the implementation of the policy.

In order to facilitate implementation of the National Policy and to bring about a qualitative improvement in the programme interventions of the Ministry both the ongoing schemes were revised during the year.

Scheme of Assistance to Panchayati Raj institutions/volunatry organisations/self help groups for construction of old age homes/ multi service centres for older persons

The Scheme of Assistance to Panchayati Raj Institutions/ Voluntary Organisations for Construction of Old Age Homes was revised and broad based. Under the revised scheme which bears the nomenclature: Scheme of assistance to Panchayati Raj Institutions/Voluntary Organisation/Self Help Groups for Construction of Old Age Homes/Multi Service Centres for Older Persons a one time grant of Rs. 30 lakhs is provided to eligible organisations.

The Scheme aims at providing financial grant for construction of old age home or Service Centre for Older

Persons. To this end a one time construction assistance shall be provided to Non-Governmental Organisation/ Self Help Groups/Panchayati Raj Institutions for construction of Old Age Home or a Multi-Service Centre consisting of Day Care Centres for the mobile; reach out units for the home bound and Old Age Homes for the destitute Older Persons.

The day Care Centres will be required to provide various non-institutional support systems to Older Persons such as developmental programmes for preparation for old age, death and bereavement; raising family and community awareness for enriched interactions; health checkup camps; information and awareness for prevention of problems and treatment; continuing education; training and opportunities for income generation, employment exchange and sponsorship; training as volunteers; recreation, cultural and creative programmes; occupational therapy, counseling and legal aid; self/mutual help groups; family assistance; information and referral services and any other programme or service in the best interest of Older Persons.

Besides Mobile Medicare the Reach out units will also run other home/family based services for home bound Older Persons such as Mobile meals, clinics, libraries; volunteer visits for help in home making and running external errands; information and referral services etc.

The Old Age Homes will provide for self fulfillment, health, nutrition and care giving, continuing education and recreation activities to the Older Persons particularly the destitute and the homless. An effort will be made to ensure that institutional life in the Old Age Homes corresponds to normal conditions in the family and in the community. To this end the homes may keep their health, education and recreation services open to non-resident Older Persons. The residents interaction with their family members and the community would also be encouraged.

Grant in aid under the scheme shall be limited to Rs. 30 lakhs per Home/Centre and this amount shall be used only for the purpose of:

(i) Construction of building and for furnishing/ equipping the old age home/multi-service centre;

(ii) Expansion of the existing building, of the existing home/centre;

(iii) Completion of the construction of the building and for furnishing/equipping the home/centre.

Grant will be released in two instalments - the first instalment not exceeding 70% will be released at the time of sanctioning of the project. The second instalment will be released on confirmation that the construction has started and has reached the plinth level. Application for release of second instalment shall be accompanied by a Statement of expenditure incurred so far by the institution/ organisation.

An integrated programme for older persons

The Scheme of Assistance to Voluntary Organisations for Programmes relating to Welfare of Aged was also similarly revised and made flexible so as to be able to meet the diverse needs of the Older Persons and it has been also given a new nomenclature: An Integrated Programme for Older Persons. The basic objective of the revised scheme are to:

(i) Reinforce and strengthen the ability and commitment of the family to provide care to Older Persons;

(ii) Foster amiable multi-generational relationships;

(iii) Generate greater awareness on issues pertaining to Older persons and enhanced measures to address these issues;

(iv) Popularise the concept of Life Long Preparation for Old Age at the individual level as well as at the societal level;

(v) Facilitate Productive Ageing;

(vi) Promote Health Care, Housing and Income Security needs of Older Persons;

(vii) Provide care to the Destitute elderly.

While the basic thrust of the programme will be on the Older Persons (of age 60, years and above) particularly the infirm, destitute and the widows amongst them, broad based interventions targeting the family and the community shall also be undertaken within the overall context of improving the quality of life of Older Persons.

Within this framework under the scheme the Ministry will provide support and financial assistance to a wide range of programmes including;

(i) Programmes to reinforce and enhance the commitment and ability of the family to take care of Older Persons;

(ii) Programmes to build and strengthen intergenerational relationships particularly between children/youth and Older Persons;

(iii) Programmes emphasising and contributing towards the need to undertake Life Long Preparation for Old Age;

(iv) Programmes facilitating Productive Ageing;

(v) Programmes enabling formation of Self Help Groups/Associations of Older Persons and advancement of their rights and interests;

(vi) Programmes facilitating and improving the Health care of Older Persons including development of trained manpower/para medicos to provide care and attention to Older Persons;

(vii) Programmes attending to the housing needs of Older Persons particularly shelter to the destitute elderly;

(viii) Programmes aimed at promoting the Income Security needs of Older Persons particularly those engaged in Agriculture, Non Formal Sector and those living in rural areas

(ix) Programmes for providing Institutional as well as Non Institutional Care/Services to Older Persons;

(x) Advocacy and Awareness building programmes in the field of Ageing;

(xi) Research, Training and Documentation in the field of Ageing; and

(xii) Any other programmes in the best interests of Older Persons.

Under the revised scheme up to 90% of the cost of the project will be provided by the Government of India and the remaining shall be borne by the organisation/institution concerned. However, in the case of schools, colleges and recognised youth organisations such as Nehru Yuvak Kendra Sanghathan (NYKS) and the National Service Scheme (NSS) undertaking programmes and services for Older Persons 100% cost of the project shall be provided by the Government. In case of State Government/Municipal Bodies undertaking execution of any activity directly the funding pattern will be 90 : 10 between the Government of India and the State Government/Local Body. However, where an activity is taken up by Union Territory Administration 100% of the cost shall be borne by the Government of India. Similarly, if the Ministry of Social Justice & Empowerment itself executes any part of the programme (Monitoring and Evaluation of the Scheme, Advocacy, Awareness building, Research, Documentation, Training etc.) full cost shall be payable from budgetary allocations made for the programme.

Under the Programme while no predefined cost heads shall be stipulated, at the project formulation stage each -implementing agency shall submit a detailed proposal clearly bringing out programme modalities and individual expenditure heads. The Ministry of Social Justice & Empowerment while approving the projects shall indicate the extent of support to the project as a whole as well as to each component of the project which shall not be variable except by prior approval of the Ministry. Normally a ceiling of Rs. 10 Lakhs per annurn per project shall be applicable for release of grants-in-aid under the programme. Further for all new projects under the scheme, there shall be a ceiling of 60% on the expenditure to be incurred by a organisation on administrative costs and the balance 40% of the expenditure must be spend directly on the beneficiaries. In exceptional cases however, deviance from these norms may be permitted by the Secretary (SJ&E).

Grants will be given in two equal instalments. The first instalment will cover 50% of the sanctioned amount and will be released on receipt of the prescribed proforma. The remaining 50% will be released as the second instalment on receipt of the prescribed proforma.

Project oasis

An Old Age Social and Income Security (OASIS) project was also launched during the year to comprehensively examine policy questions connected with Old Age Income Security. The Project OASIS Phase-I report was formally presented by the Minister for Social Justice &

Empowerment to the Finance Minister with a plan of action for enhancing the coverage and the rate of returns of the existing Social Security Instruments: Employees Provident Fund, Public Provident Fund, Pension schemes of LIC, UTI etc,

Partnership between the old and the young

Realising the importance of strengthening partnership between the young and the old a collaborative project was launched with the Nehru Yuvak Kendra Sangathan under which 100 new Day Care Centres for Older Persons were established in different parts of the country. Based upon deliberations with representatives from schools the blueprint of a programme intervention to bring school children and Older Persons together was also prepared.

New projects sanctioned during the year

As a part of the ongoing schemes of the Ministry grants-in-aid were provided to NGOs to establish 44 new Old Age Homes, 164 new Day Care Centres, 12 new Mobile Medicare Units and 1 new project for providing Non-institutional Services to the Older Persons. The Ministry is as a result supporting 230 Old Age Homes, 387 Day Care Centres, 40 Mobile Medicare Units and 3 Projects of Non-Institutional Services for Older Persons,

New performance

In order to improve the quality of feed back on performance of the projects and to ensure better utilisation of funds a new performance appraisal system will be put in place from the next financial year under which in addition to State Governments inspections will be carried out by other authorised agencies such as Schools of Social Work. It is expected that this will go a long way in ensuring full utilisation of funds as well as due to delays on the part of State Governments year after year the Ministry has not been able to use the full quantum of funds provided for the schemes for older persons. The allocation and expenditure incurred during the preceding years under the Scheme of Financial Assistance to Voluntary Organisation for Programmes related to Aged is given below:

(Rs. in lakhs)

S.No.	*Year*	*Budget*	*Expenditure Estimates*
1.	1992-93	100.00	107.00
2.	1993-94	300.00	305.62
3.	1994-95	480.00	528.50
4.	1995-96	600.00	637.05
5.	1996-97	700.00	720.00
6.	1997-98	1250.00	610.00
7.	1998-99	1500.00	640.00
			(As on 14.2.99)
	Total	4930.00	3548.85

The allocation and expenditure incurred during the preceding years under the Scheme of Assistance to Panchayati Raj Institutions/Voluntary organisations/Self Help Groups for construction of Old Age Homes/Multi Service Centres for Older Persons is given below:

(Rs. in Lakhs)

S.No.	*Year*	*Budget Estimates*	*Amounts Released*
1.	1996-97	500.00	130.00
2.	1997-98	500.00	30.00
3.	1998-99	320.00	68.84
			(As on 14.2.99)
	Total	1320.00	228.84

A statement showing release of grants in aid under the Scheme of Financial Assistance to Voluntary Organisations for Programmes relating to Welfare of Aged for ongoing projects.

A statement showing release of grants in aid under the Scheme of Financial Assistance to Voluntary Organisations for Programmes relating to Welfare of Aged for new projects.

A statement showing release of grants in aid State-wise under the Scheme of Assistance to Panchayati Raj Institutions/Voluntary Organisations/ Self Help Groups for~ Construction of Old Age Homes/Multi Service Centres for Older Persons.

Programmes for children

The Social Defence Bureau of the Ministry is responsible for initiating policies and programmes for Street Children, children of sex workers and neglected and delinquent Juveniles. The basic framework for the mandate of the Ministry for neglected and delinquent Juveniles is provided by the Juvenile Justice Act, 1986, a Central Act applicable to the whole country except the State of Jammu & Kashmir. In order facilitate implementation of the Act the Ministry has been operating the Scheme for Prevention and Control of Juvenile Social Maladjustment since 1986. Under the scheme, financial assistance is provided to State Governments to the extent of 50% for establishing and maintaining Observation Homes, Juvenile Homes, Special Homes and After Care Institutions for neglected and delinquent Juveniles. As a part of a Non Institutional approach to the problem of neglect and destitution the Ministry has been Budget Amounts operating since 1992-93 the Scheme for Welfare of EstimatesReleased Street Children. Under the scheme upto 90% cost of projects is provided as grants-in-aid to NGOs for operating out reach programmes and establishing drop-in-shelters for Street Children. In order to meet the developmental needs of children of sex workers as well as to facilitate their integration in the society the Ministry has been providing grants-in-aid to NGOs under its Scheme of Assistance to Voluntary Organisations for Providing Social Defence Services.

During the year a complete review of all the above programmes for children was undertaken. Based upon available feed back the three schemes were revised and updated.

An integrated programme for street children

The Scheme for Welfare of Street Children was updated and is now called, An Integrated Programme for Street Children. The salient features of the revised programme are as follows:

(i) The basic aim of the programme is to prevent destitution of children and facilitate their withdrawal from a life on the streets.

(ii) Under the programme a wide range of initiatives relating to street children, can be supported including those relating to shelter, nutrition, health care, sanitation and hygiene, safe drinking water, education, recreational facilities and protection against abuse and exploitation.

(iii) In addition to voluntary organisations, under the revised programme State Governments, UT Administrations, Local Bodies and educational institutions are also eligible for financial assistance.

(iv) The target group of the programme are essentially children without homes and familyties i.e. street children and children specially vulnerable to abuse and exploitation such as children of sex workers and children of pavement dwellers. The revised programme seeks to shift the focus to these children from children living in slums who have hitherto been the main beneficiaries of the programme.

(v) The programme requires participation of organisations having experience of working for children although this clause can be relaxed in special circumstances.

(vi) Up to 90% of the cost of each project will be covered by the Govt. of India although in the case of Union Territory Administrations themselves operating a project 100% cost can be covered.

(vii) While no pro-defined cost heads are stipulated as a part of the programme, at the project formulation stage each implementing agency is required to submit a detailed proposal clearly bringing out individual expenditure heads.

(viii) The maximum amount of grants in aid admissible under the project shall be Rs 15.00 lakhs per annum.

(ix) Both ongoing as well as new projects will require to be inspected and recommended by the State/UT Government or an agency authorised for the purpose by the Ministry.

(x) Grants will be released in two equal half yearly instalments. For the release of the second instalment an organisation shall be required to amongst others submit an Audited Statement of Accounts (in four parts i.e. income and expenditure, receipt and payment, balance sheet, and utilisation certificate).

(xi) For ongoing projects a transitional period of three years effective April 99 will be provided to adjust to the new programme, particularly the shift in the target group. Also under the revised programme grants in aid will be provided to them at the per capita rate of Rs 250/- per child per month. The utilisation of these grants in aid shall be left to the discretion of each individual agency. However before the new funding pattern comes into force each NGO will be required to submit a detailed proposal of the manner in which it proposes to utilise the per capita grant in aid. The NGO in its proposal shall clearly specify item wise expenditure to be incurred which shall not be changed without the prior permission of the Ministry.

(xii) In the revised programme existing stipulation regarding minimum size of each project (300 children earlier), qualifications relating to staff (BSW/MSW) an item wise allocation of grants in aid shall not be insisted upon similarly there shall not be any restriction on the cities to be covered under the programme.

It is expected that as a result of revision and board basing the scheme of the Ministry will be able to support innovative and a diverse range of initiatives in favour of children in distress.

Introduction of child line service

One of the important initiatives taken under the revised programme during the year was establishment of Child Help Line Service in a number of cities. The Child Line is 24 hour free phone service which can be accessed by dialing the number 1098 on the telephone. Child Line provides emergency assistance to the child and subsequently based upon the child's need, the child is referred to an appropriate organisation for long* term follow up and care. The service focuses on the needs of children living alone on the streets, child labourers working in the un-organised sector, domestic workers and sexually abused children.

The primary objectives of the child Line Service are:

(i) To ensure that every child in the major cities of India can avail of emergency phone assistance through the child Line Service.

(ii) To respond to children in emergency situations and refer them to relevant governmental and non-governmental organisations.

(iii) To provide a platform for networking amongst organisations and to strengthen the support systems which facilitate the rehabilitation of children in difficult circumstances through on going training to develop affective management information systems.

(iv) to, sensitize collateral agencies such as the police, hospitals, municipal corporations and the railways about the problems faced by children in difficult circumstances and to develop necessary intervention strategies.

(v) To document the process of child fine and conduct research to serve as a data bass for lobbying and advocacy on issues related to children in distress.

The Child Line is operated in each city by, a network of NGOs. For the purpose of identifying, cities for initialing the service as well as for selecting participating organisation the Ministry has engaged .the services of the Tata Instituter of Social Sciences.

In fact the design of the programme intervention itself was conceived on behalf at the Ministry by the Tata Institute of Social Sciences. This, service is currently available at Mumbai, Deft, Calcutta, Hyderabad, Nagpur, Bangalore, Chennai and, Patna Additionally preparatory-activities for Child Line have been initiated in, 13 other cities/towns across the country.

An integrated programme for juvenile justice

During the current year the, scheme for Prevention and. Control of Juvenile Social Maladjustment which the Ministry has been operating since 1986-87 was also revised with, a view to strengthening the implementation of the Juvenile Justice Act 1938 in the country and bringing about a qualitative improvement in the services provided under the scheme to both neglected as well as delinquent children. The salient features of the revised scheme which is called, "A Programme for Juvenile Justice" are as follows—

(1) Establishment of a National Advisory Board (NAB) on juvenile justice to advise the government on matters relating to the implementation of the Juvenile Justice Act 1986 in the country including the quality of infrastructure and the staff available under the Act. The Chairperson of the NAB is the Secretary. Ministry of Social Justice & Empowerment and it has representation from other Ministries of the government of India, State Governments, Juvenile Welfare Boards, Juvenile Courts, Schools of Social Work, Law Schools and NGOs.

(2) Creation of a Juvenile Justice Fund.

(3) Establishment of a Secretariat for the National Advisory Board.

(4) constitution of a Social Audit Pane (SAP) comprising of 5-6 eminent persons to report upon juvenile justice facilities in the country.

(5) Appointment of observers/to report upon implementation of the Act in different States/ UT&

(6) Institution of a Chair on Juvenile Justice at the Child and the Law Centre of the National Law School of India University, Bangalore.

(7) institution of awards for the best maintained juvenile justice institutions in each State and at the National level.

(8) Training, orientation and sensitization of judicial, administrative, police and NGO personnel

responsible for implementation of the Juvenile Justice Act 1986.

(9) Provision of 100% financial assistance to States/UTs/Voluntary Organisations to facilitate creation of infrastructure prescribed under the Act in hitherto uncovered districts of the country.

(10) Expansion of non-institutional Services such as sponsorship, foster care, probation, etc. as alternates to institutional care.

(11) Provision of scholarships to children being processed under the Act for excelling in academics or in extra curricular activities.

Partnership with the corporate sector

As a part of the Ministry's Plan of Action for strengthening and improving facilities for children a project was launched seeking participation of the Corporate Sector for providing additional facilities in observation/juvenile/special homes.

A pilot Project was initiated with the help of an external agency, Advantage India, under which a needs assessment of all the homes in Bihar and Delhi was carried out.

The possible areas of intervention and, help by the Corporate Sector in these homes were identified with the help of staff deployed in the homes. A request was thereafter sent out by the Minister for Social Justice & Empowerment to select Corporate Houses for participation in the programme.

The first home under the project has already been taken up at Delhi arid follow up action is being taken up with a number of Corporate Houses which have evinced interest in the programme.

Scheme of assistance to voluntary organisations for providing social defence dervices

The Scheme of Assistance to Voluntary Organisations for providing Social Defence Services was also revamped. Under this scheme assistance is provided for undertaking programmes which are not covered under the existing schemes of the Ministry.

In particular the scheme provides for Pilot Projects in un, chartered areas in which the Ministry may like to formulate independent programmes in due course. Under this scheme currently a number of programmes are being supported for rehabilitation of children of sex workers.

Initiatives have also been taken to support projects for rehabilitation of widows and for providing counseling and support to traumatized children and women particularly those who have been victims of physical violence and sexual abuse.

New performance appraisal system

Keeping in view the difficulties faced in obtaining inspection reports and recommendations in respect of both new and on-going projects from State Governments and to obviate the resultant delays as well as under utilisation of funds an interesting irritative taken by the bureau was relating to performance appraisal of NGOs participating in the implementation of the schemes of the Ministry.

In order to build alternate channels of feed back, the leading schools of social work in the country were contacted to undertake inspection and evaluation of the schemes for older persons and children. This programme will be operational from the next financial year.

The allocation and expenditure since the inception - of the Scheme for Welfare of Street Children is given in the next page.

(Rs. in lakhs)

S.No.	*Year*	*Budget allocation*	*Expenditure*
1.	1993-94	300.00	111.14
2.	1994-95	300.00	301.74
3.	1995-96	350.00	284.48
4.	1996-97	450.00	340.00
5.	1997-98	400.00	348.00
6.	1998-99	800.00	409.32
			(As on 14.2.99)
	Total	2300.00	1794.68

The allocation and expenditure since the inception of the Scheme of Assistance to Voluntary Organisations, for Providing Social Defence Services is given below.

(Rs. in lakhs)

S.No.	*Year*	*Budget*	*Expenditure Allocation*
1.	1992-93	50.00	57.00
2.	1993-94	50.00	22.16
3.	1994-95	25.00	25.00
4.	1995-96	38.00	36.86
5.	1996-97	38.00	35.43
6.	1997-98	38.00	31.70
7.	1998-99	200.00	40.16
			(As on 14.2.99)
	Total	439.00	248.31

National institute of social defence

The National Institute of Social Defence (NISD) is a subordinate office under the administrative control of the Ministry.

The NISD serves as the Central Advisory Body in the field of prevention of crime and treatment of offenders. The main areas covered by the Institute are juvenile justice administration, welfare of prisoners, probation and allied measures, suppression of immoral traffic, beggary control and drug abuse prevention. During the year the mandate of the institute was enlarged to cover areas of concern to older persons. A number of expert consultations were organised by the Institute both at the national and at the regional level which provided inputs to the Ministry for formulation of the National Policy for Older Persons. After lapse of more than a decade the practice of holding in house training programmes was revived and a number of programmes were organised in the areas of juvenile justice, beggary prevention, etc.

A major development in the NISD was upgradation of the Bureau of Drug Abuse Prevention into a full fledged National Centre for Drug Abuse Prevention (C-DAP). The basic activities planned for the Centre include conducting of research; establishment of a data base, evaluation of existing approaches; field testing of new and innovative approaches; documentation of scientific material; training of workers; development of information, education and communication material, etc. The CDAP held the first three month Certificate Training Course on De-addiction Counseling and Rehabilitation from 16th November 1998 to 12th February 1998 which invited participation from organisations from all over India as well as from countries of the SAARC region (Bangladesh, Maldives and Srilanka). The curriculum for the course was designed with the help of leading academics and practitioners from India arid abroad.

Realising the growing menance of drug abuse in the north eastern region of the country the NISD launched a project for Training of 'trainers on drug abuse prevention. Under the project a large number of social workers from the north east were attached for theoretical as well as practical training with 1995 leading organisations/institutions working on drug 1996 abuse prevention in the country. The trained workers 1997 are expected in turn to disseminate knowledge the subject in their respective States.

The NISD also initiated a programme to sensitize police personnel on different facets of drug abuse by providing training inputs at the police stations themselves.

A working group to review the Probation Services in the country was also constituted to suggest measures for reviving and strengthening this important crime prevention strategy.

A statement showing training programmes organised by the NISD during the current financial year.

Central adoption resource agency (CARA)

It is an accepted fact that for full fledged development of the child-emotionally, physically as well as intelectually it is desirable that the child is given an opportunity to grow within familiar surroundings. It becomes the responsibility of the community, the society and the state to provide the necessary institutional as well as non-institutional infrastructure to the orphaned, abandon relinquished, neglected and destitute children Adoption has been considered the most ideal effective medium of non-institutional rehabilitation for the children.

In India there is no uniform law on adoption. Hindus can adopt a child under the Hindu Adoption and Maintenance Act, 1956, while others can take a child under their guardianship under the Guardians and Wards Act, 1890.

The Ministry of Social Justice & Empowerment grants recognition to both Indian and foreign agencies which are engaged in sponsoring children for adoption abroad. About 85 agencies in the country have been given recognition for doing inter country adoption. In addition, 292 foreign agencies have also been enlisted to sponsor inter country adoption cases in more than 25 countries. During the last 3 year and upto September, 98 the following estimated number of children have founded home through these agencies as per records available with C.A.R.A.

Year	*In country adoptions*	*Inter country adoptions*	*Total*
1995	1424	1236	2660
1996	1623	990	2613
1997	1330	1026	2356
1998	858	665	1523
		(Sep. 98)	
Total	5235	3917	9152

Guidelines for Foster Family Care as an alternative to Institutional Care for children awaiting adoption has been circulated to Voluntary Social/Child Welfare agency and State Govts. for implementation and these Guidelines is being published in the Gazette of India 5 new agencies in India and 7 new agencies abroad have been given recognition/ enlistment by this Ministry for doing inter country adoption.

The Shishu Greh Scheme has been revised and the ceding on Grant in Aid has been raised to Rs. 6.00 lakhs in order to facilitate better services for the children. As far as the Voluntary Coordinating Agencies are concerned, there is no structured scheme and the funds are met from the General Grant in Aid Head of the Ministry where Rs. 41.5 lakhs is earmarked. The Planning Commission has agreed to examine the possibility of considering its inclusion in the Annual Plan proposals for the year 1999-2000. Pending that a separate proposal has already been sent to Internal Finance Division for revising the expenditure norms.

A total of Rs. 76.30 lakhs was provided to 23 NGOs under the Shishu Greh Scheme for the year 1997-98 in the current years, Rs. 82,87,8454 has been spent on 31 NGOs under the Scheme till 24.12.98. Further an amount of Rs. 3.30 lakhs has also been provided to 6 VCAs in the current year.

Prohibition and drug abuse prevention

The problem of drug abuse has emerged as one of the vital concerns of human race with far reaching socio-medical and economic consequences. The changes in the population structure, traditionally operative-control mechanisms and social and ethical values are closely associated with the proliferation of drug abuse in modern society. The process of industrialisation and consequential urban drift, stresses and strains of modern life have rendered individuals much more vulnerble to substance abuse than ever before.

The use of dependence-producing substances, in some form or the other, has been a universal phenomenon. In India too, the abuse of alcohol, opium and cannabis has been known for long. But, the consumption of drugs like heroin, hashish, LSD etc., is altogether a new trend. Within a decade or so, the proliferation of such lethal drugs in various segments of society seems to have acquired an alarming dimension, India, today, is no more merely as transit country for illicit trafficking in drugs from 'golden triangle' or 'golden crescent'. It is also becoming a consumer in the global scenario. As long as addiction was a problem of certain individuals or socially alienated groups and was well contained by informal social control mechanism, it did not evoke much attention. However, with its seepage and spread among various socio-cultural and economic strata and in increasing perception of its disruptive influence on the individual, the family and society at large, drug abuse has emerged as a vital issue of the quality of life and welfare of the people.

Addiction to drugs is not merely a problem for the physical and mental health of the individual involved. He also disrupts his family and social relationship. An addict is not on loss to himself but also to society as a productive individual and to the nation as an asset for development. Trend is most ominous for a developing country like India which is still struggling to overcome its basic problems of poverty, hunger and disease. Drug Abuse has emerged as a vital issue of the present and future quality of human life for us as much as for other countries.

Experience has shown that the demand' of drugs can be curbed effectively only in a social climate of abstience among the people to be created by propagating -a life style that rejects the Use of dependence producing substances. By and large, abstience is still deeply rooted, in our culture and is strongly supported by the family, the community and the religion.

In order to tackle the problem of drug abuse a two pronged strategy has been adopted by the Govt., of India i.e. (a) supply control (b) demand reduction while supply control aspect is taken care of by the Narcotic Control Bureau and the Police, the Ministry of Social Justice and Empowerment has been given the responsibilities of looking after the social welfare and educational aspects of drug addiction. In fulfilling this objective the Ministry of Social Justice and Empowerment has formulated three pronged strategy with the following components:—

(i) Building awareness and educating people about ill effects of drug abuise.

(ii) Dealing with the addicts through a well rounded up programme of motivation, counselling treatment, follow-up and social reintegration of cured drug addicts.

(iii) To impart drug abuse prevention rehabilitation training to voluntees having in view to build up an educated cadre of drug abuse control operators.

Assistance to voluntary organisations

In order to counteract the increasing demand for dependence-producing drugs, the Ministry has embarked on, since the Seventh Five Year Plan, a comprehensive scheme for Prohibition and Drug Abuse Prevention. The Scheme is implemented through voluntary organisations by providing them financial assistance on the basis of 90% of the approved expenditure. The programmes being supported through, setting of

Drug awareness, counselling and assistance centres

These centres provide community based services for awareness building, screening of addicts, counselling to addicts and their families, referral of hardcore addicts to De-addiction-cum-Rehabilitation centres and follow-up assistance to former addicts.

De-addlction-cum-rehabilitations centres

These centres provide community based services for awareness services for the identification, motivation counselling, de-addication, after care reintegration of addicts into the social mainstream. A De-addiction-cum-Rehabilitation Centre may either be a 15 bedded or a 30 bedded facility. While setting up new centres, no such two centres are to be set up within a radius of at least 15 kilometers from each other, Where there is a justification for two 15 bedded centres in the same area, a 30 bedded centre is being provided under the scheme.

De-addiction camps

To give a wider coverage the provision of deaddication camps has been made in the urban and rural areas where de-addication cum-Rehabilitation Centres have not been established yet but there is need for the service.. These camps are organised only by the organisations which are running Deaddiction-cum-Rehabilitation centres.

Awareness generation programmes

There is still a considerable degree of ignorance among the public about the illeffects of drug abuse on the individual, the family and the community. A deliberate decision has, therefore, been taken by the Ministry of Social Justice and Empowerment to step up awareness generation programmes which include holding of seminars, conferences workshops, corner meetings, essay/debate competitions, publicity through mass media etc.

Several radio and TV Programmes have been launched to create awareness about role of parents, teachers and opinion leaders in the prevention and control of drinking and drug abuse. A number of films have been produced and distributed to disseminate knowledge among the masses. Voluntary Organisations are being financially assisted to undertake educational work in various communities and target groups.

The experience gained by Voluntary Organisations in selected case studies, is being widely shared with enlightened groups to invigorate their role in educating the public and preventing drug abuse. The utilisation, of community based organisations like Youth Clubs, Religious Institutions, Planchayats, I C. D S, P H C is also being explored.

Evaluation of the programme and future thrust areas

Rehabilitation

The ultimate goal of treatment of substance abusers is to help them to enter into society so that they are able to lead healthy and productive life In other words, the objective is to achieve "Whole person recovery" (WPR) which emphasises the physical, emotional and mental rehabilitation culminating to a physically, socially and economically self-dependent life for the recovering addicts.

It is, therefore, felt imperative that rehabilitation aspect should receive more focus in the programme.

Based on the discussions in the core group set up in the Ministry comprising of professionals and representatives of international bodies, the entire scheme is being remodified with emphasis on total recovery/ rehabilitation of the addict and reducing the dependence on the large number of purely medical staff. The Ministry has now undertaken revision of the Scheme based on the past experience and interaction with the NGOs to introduce flexibility in operation, revision of financial norms and encourage innovative approaches. It is desired to solicit greater involvement of voluntary as well as Corporate Sector in implementation of the various programmes.

In order to provide a holistic treatment to the addict which will go long way in helping the rehabilitation process, the possibilities of better utilisation of Indian and traditional systems of' medicines for recovery of addicts is also actively explored A three day Workshop was held in the month of April, 1997 on this subject. Their recommendations are being examined and suitable modifications are proposed in the Scheme to enable alternative systems of medicines to be utilised for treatment of drug addicts.

Socially and economically vulnerable targets groups

Special attention is being given to tackle drug abuse problem amongst socially and economically vulnerable groups as street children, commercial sex workers, destitute women etc. In this connection, all the NGOs and State Governments are addressed for identifying these groups and the facilities that are required to be provided to them. A project on Reducing Risk Behaviors and HIV/AIDS/STD drug abuse among street children has been undertaken by the then Ministry of Welfare, United Nations Drug Control Programme, UNICEF,. WHO, NACO and ODA. City level plan have been prepared for four cities namely Bombay, Hyderabad, Calcutta and Delhi and a national Action Plan has been formulated.

Special initiatives in the north-eastern region

In consonance with, the directives of the Prime Minister cf India, special focus is given to the Drug Abuse Prevention Programme in North-East keeping in view the enormity of the problem.

A three day Workshop was conducted on Need Assessment Study of the Problem of Drug Abuse in North-East at Imphal from 29—31 January, 1697 to assess the ground realities of the problem and plan future interventions. Accordingly, a three pronged strategy has been adopted 'for the North-East.

(a) Training and enhancing the capabilities of the NGOs in the area.

(b) Extending the outreach of drug abuse prevention scheme of the Ministry by opening of new cantres; and

(c) Awareness and Education Programmes for "he North-East.

Five Training Programmes for trainers, 16 training Courses for Service Providers in the North East and

Attachment training of service providers in reputed Centres is also being implemented. A Committee has been constituted by the Ministry to visit the north

Eastern States for reviewing the working of the existing NGOs, explore the possibilities for opening of new Centres; and identify service providers for the purpose of training.

The Ministry has established a Centre for Drug Abuse Prevention under the aegis of the National Institute of Social Defence, New Delhi, a subordinate office of the Ministry to serve as the apex body in the country in the field of training, research and documentation in the field of drug abuse prevention. To meet the growing demand of rehabilitation professional in the country, the Centre has started three months Certificate course on Deaddiction Counselling and 'Rehabilitation of Drug Abusers from 16th November, 1.99.8.

Work place prevention programme

Realising that the drug and alcohol addiction amongst the workers in industries is very high, the Work Place Prevention is being given greater importance. In this connection, ILO-UNDCP/Ministry of Social Justice & Empowerment 'Project on Community Rehabilitation and Work Place is already under way for developing modules for work prevention.

Achievements

Beginning with seven Centres established in Delhi in 1985-86 the total number of Centres has reached 414 as on 31st December, 1998 of which 218 are Drug Awareness, Counselling and Assistance Centres and 196 De-addiction-cum-rehabilitation Centres. State/UT wise number of centres and voluntary organisations given grant-in-aid under the Scheme.

As a result of the impact of the implementation of the program, me the number of Drug Addicts registered in these Centres was 2.49 lakhs in 1997-98 of which about 0.90 lakhs were detoxified.

During the year 1998-99 (upto September, 1998) about 1.29 lakhs drug addicts were registered and 51,164 were detoxified in these centres.

In order to provide for better training and qualified personnel -amongst the service providers, the Ministry in collaboration with United Nations International Drug Control Programme (UNDCP), has taken up a number of projects which include Community Drug Rehabilitation and Work Place Prevention Programme.

This is in collaboration with ILO and UNDCP. Under this programme, 20 NGOs have been identified in different parts of the country with an objective to train at least 4000 service providers in rehabilitation of drugs.

Another study was conducted on Reducing Risk Behavior relating to HIV/AIDS/STD Drug Abuse among Street Children sponsored by the Ministry of Social Justice and Empowerment, WHO, UNDCP, UNICEF and Ministry of Health and Family Welfare. City level action plans have been prepared for 4 cities viz. Bombay, Calcutta, Hyderabad and Delhi and a National Action Plan have been formulated.

In order to have an exhaustive data regarding the extent of drug abuse problem in the country, the Ministry proposes to take up an extensive survey on the drug abuse scenario in India which interalia will also include a survey on the HV/AIDS infected IDUs for facilitating better planning in future.

Year	*BE (Rs. in crores)*	*Expenditure (Rs. in crores)*	*No. of centres*	*No. of Addicts registered*	*No. of Addicts Detoxified*
1	2	3	4	5	6
1992-97 (VIII Plan)	70.25				
1992-93	6.92	8.06	254	270133	85115
1993-94	7.60	9.87	274	290623	101007
1994-95	14.00	13.50	376	312113	110858
1995-96	15.00	11.00	363	282266	107328
1996-97	14.50	9.57	341	305098	114831
IXth Plan	17.50				
1997-98	(RE 11.52)	11.52	370	249048	90050
1998-99	16.00	11.26 (31st Dec.,) 1998		129639 (upto Sept., 1998)	51164 (Upto Sept., 1998)

Monitoring system

Monitoring forms an integral part of the Scheme. The programme is evaluated on the basis of information and statistics collected in prescribed proforme on quarterly and yearly basis from the De-addiction and counselling Centres funded by the Ministry. The feed back enables the Ministry to evaluate the performance of the voluntary agencies. The State Government conducts yearly inspection of the agencies and sends its report to the Ministry of Social Justice & Empowerment.

The grantee organisations are required to 'furnish Utilisation Certificate and audited accounts verified by Chartered Accountant. The second instalment to the NGO is released only on the basis of the Inspection Report and recommendation of the State Government. In order to undertake regular review of the progress of utilisation of funds under the Scheme, Ministry of Social Justice & Empowerment has convened series of meetings with State/UT Social Welfare Secretaries in November, 1997 wherein the need for a proper and intensive evaluation of the working of the Centres was stressed.

15

Information and Mass Education

The concept of Welfare State as enshrined in the constitution finds emphatic expression in its preamble and Directive Principles of State Policy. These envisage a positive role for the State in bringing about the Welfare and Development of disadvantaged and marginalised groups of society. Through successive plans socio-economic programmes have been aimed at improving and uplifting the economic conditions of the people. In order to bring the goals of economic and social development to the weaker sections of the society a number of programmes have been grown up by the Government and concerted efforts have been made for their upliftment.

Media strategy

The Ministry of Social Justice and Empowerment undertakes a large number of Welfare activities and schemes for the social disadvantaged, weaker and marginalised sections of society which include Scheduled Castes, Scheduled Tribes, minorities, the Other Backward Classes, Handicapped, destitute children, the aged, Drug addicts, alcoholics, beggars, Animal welfare etc. There is need to give wide publicity to the various schemes being implemented by this Ministry for awareness and education of the masses. The information and Mass Education Cell in the Ministry caters to this vital need.

The above objective is sought to be achieved through multi media publicity campaign. The programmes in this regard are developed through mass media including radio, video spots/quickies films, advertisements, print material, plays, ballets, village folk dances etc.

Objectives

The specific objectives of the programme are:-

(i) To inform and educate the public regarding various welfare schemes sponsored by the Ministry of SJ&E for various sections of the society.

(ii) To promote positive social attitude which is condusive to better care growth and development.

(iii) To produce educative material and develop to appropriate aids for reaching out to the specific targets and risk groups.

In view of the large number of sensitive subjects being dealt by this Ministry, the need for an appropriate multi-media campaign for prohibition, Drug Abuse Prevention, Welfare of the SCs/STs. Backward Classes, Minorities, Handicapped, Animal Welfare etc. will have to be continued and intensified with the objective of following for these sections.

The Planning Commission in the plan document relating to the Social Defence sector has made a categorical mention about the need for enlargement of the role of the media with regard to the various programmes dealing with the socially vulnerable sections of the society. This would require a Manifold stepping up in the publicity activities of this Ministry.

The various schemes and achievements of this Ministry are publicised through a Multi-Media campaign consisting following media—

Radio

(1) 10 mts. Drama based radio sponsored Programme "Aao Haath Badhayen" entered the thirteenth year of its broadcast during 1998-99. 52 Programmes have been produced in Hindi and eleven regional languages on welfare of schemes for weaker and disadvantaged sections of the society. These are broadcast over 30 commercial channels (Vividh Bharati) of AIR throughout the year and 26 programmes have been produced and broadcast over 15 prime channels of North East in 8 NE region languages w.e.f. October, 1998.

(2) Coverage of Social Development Fair 12-20 May, 1998.

(3) Pannel discussion on Drug Abuse Prevention through All India Radio on 26.6.97.

(4) Coverage of Cultural Programme on the occasion of International Day against Drug Abuse and illicit trafficking.

(5) Radio varta, Radio talk on Drug Abuse Prevention on Occasion of International day against Drug Abuse & Illicit Trafficking.

(6) Film on 'Ability India Exhibition, 1998' was produced.

(7) Coverage of 'Ability India Exhibition' on Disability in September, 98 at Pragati Maidan, New Delhi.

(8) Pannel discussion on Disability on 3.12.98.

(9) Radio Varta on Disability on 3.12.98

(10) Coverage of National Award function was done over AIR on - the occasion of International Day for the Disabled Persons (3.12-97)

(11) Coverage of Cultural function of reception of Tribal guests and Tableau Artists on 31st January 1999.

Films/video

(1) Coverage of Social Development Fair, 1998.

(2) Film "Apnapan" on adoption was produced.

(3) Film "Ehasas", Dushman Dost, Sankalp, Mrigtrishna, Yesterday's addict today's counsellor, Paigam Wapsika were telecast on National network w.e.f. 15.6.98 to 30.6.98.

(4) Coverage of cultural Programme through Doordarshan, Zee TV, NDTV, Aaaj Tak on the occasion of International Day against Drug Abuse and Illicit Trafficking (26.6.98).

(5) Coverage of Ability India Exhibition organised at Pragati Maidan in September, 98.

(6) Curtain Raiser on International Day for the Disabled, 98 on 2nd December, 98.

(7) Live Coverage of National Award Function was~ done over National Channel (DD-1) on the occasion of International Day for the Disabled, 98.

(8) Video spots and films on various disabilities were telecast over DD 1, DD 11 and DD III free of cost, w.e.f. , 31st November to 15th December, 1998.

(9) Film Bhor-Bhai on-Disability was screened in theatres in December, 1998.

(10) Coverage of Exhibition in Handicraft items produced by Disabled persons through Doordarshan.

(11) Film 'Apnapan' on adoption was telecast over National channel in January, 98.

(12) Film 'Arpan' and 'Glani' on Drug Abuse Prevention and 'Hamari Beti' on Adoption was produced and telecast over DD I and DD It 5 times.

(13) 13 films on various themes of the Ministry were produced.

(14) One Full length film titled 'SAMAR'- on Dalit Empowerment was produced and screened twice, once for Ministry Official and once for forum of SC/ST Parliamentarian in Siri Fort Auditorium and Films Division Auditorium.

(15) coverage 'of Cultural function of reception of Tribal guests and Tableau Artists on 31st January, 98.

Print media

(1) Slogans/Messages on untouchability, Disability, Scheduled Caste development, Drug Abuse Prevention, Care of the Aged, Adoption, antibeggary and prohibition were printed throughout the year on the following items:-

(i) Computerised Railway tickets on Northern and Eastern Railway.

(ii) Postal stationery i.e. Inland cards. Post cards, Aero Grammes and POSB Pass Books.

(2) Two Booklets on Scheduled Caste Development were printed and distributed.

(3) Posters, Booklets, Leaflets, Folders on Drug Abuse Prevention, adoption and older persons were printed and Distributed in Social Development fair, 98 NGOs,

(4) Leaflet on Drug Abuse Prevenion, adoption and older persons were printed and distributed.

(5) Folder on adoption was Printed and distributed.

(6) 2nd issue of News letter on Disability was released.

Out door media

Messages/slogans on various social welfare issues were on continuous display through the following media–

a. Social Development Fair was organised at pragati Maidan, New Delhi in the Month of May, 98 to publicise the activities of the Ministry.

b. Four cultural evenings were organised during Social Development Fair, 98 for minority and Backward Classes, Disability, scheduled Caste Development and Social Defence Divisions.

c. 8 animation display on themes of Handicapped welfare, Drug Abuse Prevention, prohibition, Care of the Aged, Anti beggary and adoption at Katra in Jammu.

d. 187 Hoardings on Drug Abuse Prevention in Delhi, Pondicherry, Madhya Pradesh, Rajasthan and North Eastern Region.

e. 450 Kiosks on Drug Abuse Prevention and Untouchability in Jaipur, Faridabad, Calcutta, Mumbai, Allahabad, Jalandhar, Ghaziabad.

Press media

(1) One full page advertisement on Dr. B.R. Ambedkar was released on the occasion of birth anniversary of Baba Saheb.

(2) 2 quarter page advertisement released in Hindi and English on Social Development Fair, 1998.

(3) One advt. on National Award for Handicapped welfare was released in National Dailies and Regional News Papers in Hindi, English and Regional languages.

(4) One full page News Paper Supplement on the occasion of International Day against Drug Abuse and Illicit Trafficking (26.6.98) released in Hindi, English and regional languages.

(5) Three quarter page advt. on ability India Exhibition were released all over India In English, Hindi and regional languages in September, 98.

(6) One advertisement on P-re-examination coaching facility for SC/ST students was released in Hindi, English and regional languages on all India basis.

(7) One advertisement on overseas scholarship was released in Hindi, English and regional languages.

(8) One full page News paper supplement was released on the occasion of International day for the disabled persons 97 released in English Hindi and regional languages papers.

(9) One quarter advertisement was released all over India in English, Hindi and regional languages on the occasion of Mahaparinirvan Diwas of Dr. B.R. Ambedkar on 6th December, 98.

(10) Quarter page advertisement was released on reception of Tribal guests and Tableau Artists in January, 1998.

(11) One Quarter page advertisement was released all over India in English, Hindi and regional languages on provisions of 'breading of and Experiments on Animals (Control and supervision Rules 1998).

16

Social Welfare Research/Evaluation and Publications

Under the Scheme of Grant-in-aid Rules for Research & Publications, financial assistance is provided to meet the minimum necessary cost to University Departments, research institutions and professional bodies to undertake research/evaluation studies in the field of social policy, social development and social welfare.

However, the priority within these areas is given to evaluate/ assess the efficacy of the on-going programmes to have feed back on weaknesses/strengths of the programme on their implementation to assess emerging new social problems for formulation of new programmes to meet the challenges.

The assistance is also provided to organise workshops/seminars to disseminate research findings and social situation analysis likely to help in planning, programming and review of implementation. . To a limited extent assistance is also available for publication of manuscripts helpful for the development of concepts/ views in the broader areas of social welfare.

There is a Research Advisory Committee (RAC) on Social Welfare under the Chairmanship of Additional Secretary (SJ & E). It comprises nonofficial members from relevant fields such as social scientist, researchers/ eminent scholars and administrators of concerned Ministries/Departments, i.e. Ministry, Registrar General of India, Central Statistical Organisation, Planning Commission as official members.

The Committee advises on (i) identifying priority areas for research & evaluation; (ii) examination of research proposals for sponsorship; (iii) utilization of research findings of research studies sponsored by the Ministry; and (iv) other related matters.

From 1973-74 till December 98, 361 research/_ evaluation -studies have been sponsored covering wide range of subjects i.e. Disabled Welfare, Social Defence, Minorities and Other Backward Classes, social work education and having child welfare, welfare of the aged, etc. Out of these, reports in respect of 318 completed research projects have been received.

During the year (April to December, 1998), 8 research projects have been completed and the final reports received. A large number of research proposals were received from various institutions/university departments. Out of these 30 research proposals were placed in the RAC meetings held on 22nd July, 98 and 17th December, 98 for consideration.

The Committee approved 25 research projects in principle with some suggestions for modification on subjects concerning to Social Defence, Backward Classes and Disabled Welfare. In addition, financial assistance was provided to organise 2 seminars/workshops.

A budget (Plan) provision of Rs. 50 lakhs was provided-under the Scheme of Grant-in-aid Rules for Research and Publications during 1998-99. Out of this, an expenditure to the tune of Rs. 12.6 lakhs has been incurred till December, 98.

PREM Division also undertook Plan coordination with all the Programme Units of the Ministry and prepared following documents—

(i) Annual Action Plan 1998-99

(ii) Annual Plan 1998-99

(iii) Annual Report 1997-98

(iv) Annual Plan Proposal 1999-2000

Regular review meetings were organised to monitor the progress of expenditure and status of revision of schemes. The meetings proved very useful in resolving the number of pending issues and taking remedial measures for utilising the allocated funds to this Ministry.

17

Animal Welfare

The work relating to the Prevention of Cruelty to Animals Act, 1960 (59 of 1960) and Prevention of Cruelty to Animals was transferred to the Ministry of Social Justice & Empowerment from the Ministry of Environment and Forests on 3rd September, 1998.

Besides persuing the on-going activities for animal welfare, the Ministry of Social Justice and Empowerment has taken various steps for prevention of cruelty to animals. A fresh notification was issued on 14th October, 1998 specifying that Bears, Monkeys, Tigers, Panthers and Lions shall not be exhibited or trained as perforing animals. With a view to make provisions of Prevention of Cruelty to Animals Act, 1960 more effective to deal with the offenders, the Ministry has initiated necessary steps to amend the Act.

The following two new schemes have been framed and implemented from this year:

(i) Scheme for provision of Ambulance Services to animals in distress.

(ii) Scheme for provision of Shelter Houses for looking after Animals.

The basic objective of the scheme for provision of

Ambulance services to animals in distress is to make available emergency services to animals in distress throughout the country by provision of appropriate assistance to competent organisations working in the field. The budget provision for this scheme for 199899 is Rs. 2.50 crore.

The objective of the scheme for provision of Shelter Houses for looking after animals is to make provision for establishment and maintenance of shelter houses in all the districts of the country for care and protection of the animals. The components of the scheme include construction of shelter houses, construction of small health care centre for each shelter house, construction of water troughs and purchase of medical equipments. Under this scheme grants can be given to voluntary organisations/ institutions, universities, research institutes, schools, statutory bodies like Panchayat Raj Institutions, Municipal Corporations, Town Area Committees, Red Cross Societies and its branches. Rs 2.50 crore has been provided for this scheme for 1998-99.

The Planning Commission have further approved the following schemes for inclusion in this Ministry' Plan*.-

i) Birth Control and Immunization of stray dogs.

ii) Setting up a National Institute of Animal Welfare.

iii) Scholarship to the students for studies Abroad in Animal Welfare.

Animal Welfare Fortnight was celebrated from 14th January, 1999 to Martyr's day.

Efforts are being made to establish SPCAs in all the districts of the country.

The Breeding of and Experiments on Animals (Control & Supervision) Rules 1998 were notified in the

Gazette of India (Extraordinary) dated 15.12.1998. The steps are being taken to establish an office for the Committee for Control and Supervision of Experiments on Animals.

Animal Welfare Board of India, is given financial assistance for furthering its activities. During current financial year, Rs. 470.00 lakh has been released to the Board.

18

Use of Official Language Hindi

To monitor the statutory obligations and implementation of Official Language Policy of the Government, the Ministry has a Hindi Unit working under a Deputy Director (Official Language) assisted by One Assistant Director (Official language).

During the period under report this Unit which is also looking after the translation work continued its efforts to accelerate the implementation of the Official Language Policy with particular reference to the Annual Programme, 1998-99 issued by the Deptt. of Official Language which was circulated among all the officers and Sections/Divisions of the Ministry as also to all the Attached and Subordinate offices of the Ministry.

The Official Language Implementation Committee of the Ministry headed by the Joint Secretary (Admn.) which is required to hold its meeting once in every quarter, met regularly. The Committee made an assessment of the actual position regarding use of Official Language in various Divisions/Sections of the Ministry and suggested measures for removing the difficulties experienced at the working level Similar Committees have also been set up in most of the offices under the Ministry.

In pursuance of the standing instructions to the effect that all officials are required to be trained in Hindi, all the officers of the Ministry have the working knowledge of Hindi. Efforts were made during the year to nominate more and more employees for training in Hindi (Prabodh, Praveen and Pragya Classes) and also in Hindi stenography and Hindi typing under the Hindi Teaching Scheme of the Ministry of Home Affairs. All offices under the Ministry made sincere efforts to attain the targets fixed by the Deptt. of Official Language.

To enhance the use of Hindi, out of 137 typewriters in the Ministry, the number of Devanagari typewriters is 26. Besides, the Ministry has 20 billingual electronic typewriters and 24 computers have Hindi Software. As a result of provision of FAX machines in the Ministry and its offices, Hindi correspondence has further picked up as FAX messages in Hindi are sent by the Ministry frequently. As a result of the concerted efforts all papers/ documents under Section 3(3) of the Official Language Act were issued in both Hindi and English and letters received in Hindi are invariably replied to in Hindi.

"Hindi Fortnight" was organised in the Ministry from Ist to 15th September, 1998 to encourage official work in Hindi. During the fortnight a series of competitions like Essay writing. Typing, Noting and Drafting in Hindi were organised for Hindi speaking and non-Hindi speaking employees and as many as 20 winners were awarded cash prizes. One Hindi Workshop was organised exclusively for officers on 9th and 10th September, 1998 and 50 copies of "Karyalaya Sahayika" were distributed free of cost among the officers of the Ministry. Main function was hold-on 14th September, 1998 i.e. "Hindi Day" in which messages of Hon'ble Home Minister and Hon'ble Minister of State for Social Justice & Empowerment were read over to all the officers/ employees in the presence of Secretary (SJ&E).

The First Sub-Committee of the Committee of Parliament on Official Language inspected the main Secretariat of the Ministry on 11 Feb., 1999 with a view to assess the progress of the Official Language Policy of the Government.

During the period under Report, Radio sponsored programmes "Aao Hath Badbayen" was sponsored in Hindi, Films, spots and hoardings were displayed in Hindi. Messages and slogans of the Ministry were got printed in Hindi on the Railway tickets, Post Cards, Inland letters, Aerograms, Post Office Pass Books. A feature film "Samar" directed by a renowned and well acclaimed film personality Shri Shyam Benegal based on the theme of Dalit empowerment has been produced in Hindi by the Ministry.

19

General Administration

The Ministry of Welfare was constituted on 25th September, 1985 by integrating subjects of (i) Welfare of Scheduled Castes, Schedules Tribes, Religious- and Linguistic Minorities, Socially and Educationally Backward Classes (ii) Welfare of Disabled and Programmes off Social Defence, relating to the victims of alcoholism, drug addiction, juvenile social maladjustment, welfare of prisoners, children in need for care and protection, welfare of aged; (iii) matters relating to the Administration of Wakf.

The work of animal welfare has also been transferred to this ministry from Ministry of Environment & Forest since 8.9.98. With a vision to empower the downtrodden sections of the society symbolically the Ministry has been renamed as Ministry of Social Justice & Empowerment since 25.5.98.

With the constitution of 12th Lok Sabha the Ministry has be under the charge of Smt. Maneka Gandhi since 18.3.98. Shri D.K. Manavalan is serving as Secretary to the Ministry since 4.2.98.

The work of the Ministry is carried out in six major areas, each headed by a Bureau Head. The Integrated Finance Wing is headed by the Financial Adviser.

In order to computerise the functioning of the Ministry, Lap Top computers have been provided to senior level officers of the level of Joint Secretaries and above with Net working facilities. All other Officers upto the level of Section Officers have been provided computers to enable them to discharge their official duties in a more efficient manner.

Article 338 of the Constitution was amended by the Constitution (Sixty Fifth Amendment) Act, 1990, replacing the Commissioner for Scheduled Castes and Scheduled Tribes by, the National -Commission for Scheduled Castes and Scheduled Tribes. In order to evaluate the working of the various safeguards provided in the Constitution for the protection of the Minorities and to make recommendations with a view to ensure effective implementation and enforcement of all the safeguards, the Minorities Commission was set up in 1978.

On 17.5.1993, the National Commission for Minorities replaced the erstwhile Minorities Commissioner under the National Commission for Minorities Act, 1992. The new Commission is a statutory body and has the powers, of the Civil Court. The National Commission for Safai Karmacharis was set up on 12th Aug., 1994 under the National Commission for Safai Karmacharis Act, 1993.

The National Commission for Backward Classes Act, 1993 was enacted by Parliament to provide for setting up a permanent body at the centre to review the list of Other Backward Classes (OBCs) in accordance with the directions of Hon'ble Supreme Court. The Recommendations of the Commission would ordinarily be binding on the Government. The National Commission for Backward classes was constituted on 14.8.1993.

The office of Chief Commissioner for persons with disabilities was set up on 1st September, 98 as provided in the persons with disabilities (Equal opportunities, protection of rights and full participation) Act 1995. The Commissioner for Linguistic Minorities investigates all matters relating to the safeguards provided for linguistic minorities under the constitution and reports to the President upon these matters at such intervals as the President may direct.

The Ministry has under its administrative control the following Public Sector Companies:-

(a) Artificial Limbs Manufacturing corporation of India Ltd. (ALIMCO), Kanpur manufacturing aids and appliances for the disabled;

(b) National Scheduled Castes and Scheduled Tribes Finance Development Corporation, (NSFDC)

(c) National Backward Classes Finance and Development Corporation (NBCFDC)

(d) National Minorities Development and Finance Corporation (NMDFC)

(e) National Handicapped Finance and Development Corporation.

(f) National Safai Karmacharis Finance Development Corporation;

Apart from these, the Tribal Cooperative Marketing Development Federation (TRIFED) of India is working as an apex body for ensuring remunerative prices for minor forest and agriculture products of the tribals and to protect them from exploitation by private traders.

The National Institute of Social Defence, a subordinate office under the Ministry is serving as an advisory body in the field of prevention of crime and treatment of offenders, in the area of juvenile justice administration, welfare of prisoners, probation and allied measures, beggary control and drug abuse prevention.

In addition the following Institutes are working in the field of welfare of the handicapped:-

(g) National Institute for the Visually Handicapped (NIVH) Dehradun;

(h) National institute for the Orthopaedically Handicapped (NIOH) Calcutta

(i) Ali Yavar Jung National Institute for the Hearing Handicapped (NIHH), Bombay;

(j) National Institute for the Mentally Handicapped (NIMH), Secunderabad.;

(k) National Institute of Rehabilitation, Training and Research (NIRTAR), Cuttack, and

(l) Institute for Physically Handicapped, (IPH)

Dr. Ambedkar Foundation was set up as registered society under the Societies Registration Act, 1860 w.e.f 24.3.1992 in order to promote the ideas and ideals of Baba Saheb B.R. Ambedkar under the, Chairmanship of the then Welfare Minister.

In pursuance of directions of the Supreme Court, a Central Adoption Resource Agency (CARA) was set up w.e.f. 25th April, 1990. This agency acts as a clearing house of information in regard to children available for in-country and inter-country adoption and to regulate, monitor and develop programmes for the rehabilitation of children through adoption and guardianship.